Out of Order:

When Parents Journey Through Child Loss

An Anthology

Foreword: Dr. Chlorine Wimberly
Authors: Brigitte Jackson
Willie Jackson
Ernie Cason
Ronna Cason
Ruby Bostic
Rashon Itson
Afterword: Dimyas Perdue

Printed in the United States.

UBUNTU PRESS
An Imprint of Exponential EduVentures, LLC
PO BOX 7238 Dearborn, MI 48121
Fax: (866) 279-4589
www.ubuntupress.com

DEDICATION

This book is dedicated to our children who are no longer here physically but continue to warm our hearts daily with precious memories.

CONTENTS

ACKNOWLEDGMENTS

Ubuntu Press is so grateful to all the contributors to this profound anthology on grieving, where each author has bravely shared their unique journey of loss and healing. These heartfelt stories carry messages of hope and resilience, offering consolation to those who have also experienced the unimaginable pain of losing a child. Each contributor's willingness to be transparent and vulnerable underscores their commitment to helping others navigate the complex emotions of grief.

Throughout these pages, you will find an array of experiences composed and put together by individuals who have not only endured profound sorrow but have also found ways to transform their pain into sources of strength. Their stories witness the human spirit's capability to endure and seek meaning in the face of tragedy. We hope this anthology will serve as a beacon of light for those grieving, reminding them that they are not alone.

Finally, we would be remiss if we didn't honor the memory of each loved one discussed in this book who left us. We will continue to live life fully in their memory and honor what they contributed to our families.

Thank you to all the patron supporters who blessed us and encouraged us by ordering a book before its launch. Only a few of the names are listed here, but many more were supportive but did not necessarily have to be publicly acknowledged. Thank you again; your backing was inspirational.

Pre-Sale Patrons:
Lillian Winrow
Derrick Winrow
Jen Baxter
Breyanna Miner
Roger Tafoya
Michael Jackson Jr.
Dionne Thomas
Spiceda Jackson
eXfinancial CPA, Inc.
Doris (Wilson) Cannon
Anthony Bostic, Sr.
Brad Summers
Trisa Summers
Monique Glenn
Pastor John Strickling, MA
Sondra Ray
SDG Coaching/Consulting
Kimberlee Walker
David Blackmon
Marie Blackmon
Robin Cromwell-Smith
Kimberlee Walker
Kelley Walker
Melissa Wallace
Jeraldine Smith
Rev. Dr. Darrell Watson,
Emanuel CME Church
Exponential EduVentures
Married Into Crazy
Perdue Leadership
IRISE Counseling Services

FOREWORD

Being raised in the Christian faith, we're taught that God is a God of order. Nothing happens that He does not allow – God is "never caught off guard." Ecclesiastes 3:1 tells us, ***"To every thing there is a season, and a time to every purpose under the heaven"*** (KJV). Everything that happens to us is done under His purview.

This teaching is crucial to the core tenets of our faith because it provides reassurance that whatever is going on in the world or in our lives, we have comfort that while in the midst of our trials and tribulations, "someone is in control." We believe that according to Jeremiah 29:11, ***"there is an expected end."***

We sit in the congregation while the pastor says that according to Romans 8:28, ***"And we know that all things work together for good to them that love God, to them who are the called according to his purpose."*** After hearing this enlightening message, we leave the church and go home feeling better about our circumstances.

The "irony" (if you will) to all of this is that "life" has a tendency to throw us many "curve balls." "Events" occur that we often don't see coming. We "swing" at that curve ball and try to knock it out of the park. However, it seems as though many times, we "swing and miss." There may be times when we get flustered in our "game of life" and "strike out."

Participating in our "game" can leave us bewildered, flustered, or exasperated. We "see the ball" when it leaves the pitcher's hand, but at the last minute, that "ball curves" away from us, and we swing and miss. It may not seem fair to us, and if we're not careful, we mismanage how to manage these feelings.

"Out of Order," written by several authors, broaches the difficult topic of dealing with the grief of burying our loved ones. In our society, it is generally understood that the child is to bury the parent – not the other way around. The parents often ask themselves, "How/why was this order disrupted?" "My child had their whole life ahead of them." This inverse reality thrust upon a parent can shatter one's psyche, emotions, and mental well-being.

This book provides a practical, honest, and insightful approach to dealing with the grief of burying a child. While each author speaks from personal experience, they also provide guidelines that I believe are beneficial to someone who has to deal with the same unfortunate circumstance (or perhaps you may be tasked with giving empathy to someone else).

Dealing with the "curve balls of life" will be challenging. It will sometimes be difficult - we may even feel life is unfair. There is no foresight into the future or Marty McFly and Doc with a time machine built from a remodeled DeLorean. No genie will grant you three wishes to come true. There is no easy answer. We all have a "cross to bear," a journey to traverse, and a testimony to share.

Whatever the will of God, we must believe that God's Word is true, ***"We are troubled on every side, yet not distressed; we are perplexed, but not in despair; Persecuted, but not forsaken; cast down, but not destroyed;"*** (2 Corinthians 4:8-9).

Dr. Chlorine F. Wimberly

Dr. Chlorine F. Wimberly, LCSW, MSW
President and CEO of IRISE Counseling Services, LLC
Email: cfwimberly@yahoo.com

Dr. Wimberly is a clinical social worker and therapist who specializes in domestic violence, grief, and spiritual counseling. Her services are available on Psychology Today.

INTRODUCTION

In life, there's no pain quite like a parent mourning the loss of their child. It's a wound that pierces to the core, an ache that fills every part of who you are. For the writers of this book, this anguish isn't just a distant concept—it's a stark reality etched into their very souls. They are united not merely by words on a page but by the searing agony of losing their children suddenly and without warning. They became a community of shared sorrows.

Picture the knock on the door by a loved one, the police officer confirming what you watched on the news, the doctor saying, "I'm so sorry but…," or the phone call in the dead of night—the instant when the world as you know it fractures irreparably. These authors intimately understand that moment. They've lived through, grappled with, and endured the long, lonely nights when sleep evaded them.

Every narrative within these pages serves as a witness to resilience—a tribute to the indomitable human spirit's ability to withstand the unimaginable. From the crushing loss of a child to the unyielding grip of grief, these narratives lay bare the raw, unfiltered reality of parental bereavement. Yet, during the moments of tears and heartache, a glimmer of hope persists—a beacon of light guiding the way toward healing and restoration, showing you that you, too, can find strength in your journey.

You Are Not Alone

You're not alone on this journey through grief. It's easy to feel at times like nobody understands the depth of your pain, but within the pages of this book, you'll find a community of parents who have walked a similar path. Each story is unique, yet the threads of shared sorrow and solidarity weave it together.

These parents know firsthand the challenges of waking up each morning with a heavy heart, facing the day with a sense of emptiness that seems to linger. They understand the rollercoaster of emotions—the sadness, the guilt, the confusion, the anger, and the profound ache accompanying loss.

But despite the darkness, there is light to be found in the company of others who have passed through this difficult landscape. In sharing their experiences, these parents offer not only solace but also the reassurance that healing is possible. Together, we can lean on one another for support, finding strength in our shared humanity and resilience in our collective journey.

The Power of Memory and Meaning

Memories are like a special bookshelf in your mind. They hold all the stories of your life—the good times, the laughs, and the love. But when you lose someone you love, those memories can feel like a double-edged sword. In the wake of loss, your memories can become a battleground. They offer moments of fleeting comfort, reminding you of the good times you shared, the laughter you enjoyed, and the bond that will never be broken. But they also carry with them the weight of your grief, the sharp sting of absence, the ache of longing for one more hug, one more smile, one more chance to say goodbye.

Your memories are not frozen in time. They can change over time, like a story you rewrite as you grow and heal. This ability to change and adapt is what we call being flexible—it's like bending without breaking, finding strength even in tough times.

Think of it like a tree swaying in the wind. When the storm comes, the tree doesn't snap—it bends and flexes to withstand the force of the wind. In the same way, when you face challenges in life, your ability to be flexible helps you cope and find strength.

Being flexible doesn't mean forgetting or ignoring your pain. It means holding your memories gently, allowing them to change and evolve as you heal. It's like permitting yourself to feel your emotions without letting them overwhelm you.

As you journey through grief, your memories become more than just pictures in your mind. They become tools for healing. You learn to hold them gently, like precious gifts, instead of heavy burdens. And through this process, you find meaning and purpose in your pain.

Your memories guide you through the tough times, helping you find your way back to hope. They remind you that even though things may seem dark, there's always a light to lead you forward.

So, embrace your memories, even when they hurt. Honor the past while looking toward the future. And remember that your memories are what make you who you are—they're your story, your strength, and your hope.

The Gap and The Gain: Finding Meaning

In the book of the same name, Dan Sullivan and Ben Hardy introduce the transformative concept of "The Gap and The Gain" in an insightful exploration of human psychology and personal development. At its core, this concept is about reframing our perception of challenges and setbacks, recognizing that within every adversity lies the seed of opportunity.

Imagine standing on the edge of a broad valley, gazing into the darkness below. This is the Gap—the space between where we are and where we want to be, between our current reality and our desired outcome. It's a place of uncertainty and discomfort, where fear and doubt can easily take root. But here's the thing about the Gap: it's also where the magic happens. It's where we find the fuel for growth and transformation and discover hidden reserves of strength and resilience that we never knew we possessed. It's where we learn to control the power of adversity and turn it into a catalyst for positive change.

Now, let's talk about Gain—the other side of the equation, the light at the end of the tunnel. Gain is what we achieve when we bridge the Gap, overcome obstacles, and emerge on the other side stronger, wiser, and more empowered than before. Gain measures the progress from where we were to where we are currently. It's the lessons learned, the wisdom gained, and the personal growth that comes from facing life's challenges head-on.

So, how does this relate to the journey of parental bereavement? Or any bereavement, for that matter. How can we apply the principles of the Gap and the Gain to the profound loss of a child (or family member)?

In the aftermath of loss, it's easy to get stuck in the Gap—to become mired in despair and hopelessness, unable to see beyond the darkness surrounding us. But within that darkness lies the potential for growth and transformation. In the moments of most profound sorrow, we often find our greatest strength, our most bottomless reservoirs of resilience.

By reframing our perception of grief, by viewing it not as an insurmountable obstacle but as a catalyst for personal growth, we can begin to see the Gain—the lessons learned, the love shared, and the legacy left behind by our beloved children. We can find meaning during madness, strength in vulnerability, and hope in the face of despair.

This book proves the power of "The Gap and The Gain" - to the transformative potential of reframing our perception of grief and loss. It is a roadmap of examples of navigating parental bereavement, a guidebook for finding light in the blackness and hope in despair.

As you journey through these pages, I encourage you to embrace the principles of "The Gap and The Gain" - to view your grief not as a burden to be borne but as a journey to be welcomed. For within the depths of your sorrow lies the potential for growth and transformation, for healing and wholeness beyond measure. That may sound easier said than done, and it is at times; trust me, I know firsthand. But nothing beats walking in the Gain.

My great aunt, Irene's story, is a prime example of this truth of the Gain and the embracing of the journey. In our darkest hours, we often discover reservoirs of strength we never knew we possessed. In 1952, tragedy struck Aunt Irene's family when a devastating house fire claimed the lives of all seven of her children. The pain she and Uncle Frank must have endured is beyond comprehension, with the youngest just a babe and the eldest a mere twelve years old.

Aunt Irene could have easily been consumed for a lifetime by the overwhelming grief—the gaping chasm of despair known as the Gap. How long she dwelled in that shadowy void, I cannot say. However, as a child growing up in the 1960s and 1970s, I witnessed something remarkable. Despite the unimaginable loss, I saw her unwavering devotion to God and a steadfast commitment to hope—the essence of the Gain.

Instead of allowing despair to define her life, Aunt Irene chose a different path illuminated by faith, resilience, and unwavering hope. She turned her pain into purpose, her sorrow into strength, and her loss into a legacy of love. In doing so, she became a beacon of inspiration for all who knew her in the community, a living witness to the transformative power of resilience and faith.

The Lens of Grief and Behavior Styles

Understanding our behavioral preferences can provide invaluable insight into how we process and cope with loss. Three of the contributors of this book, Ernie Cason, Dimyas Perdue, and Brigitte Jackson, are certified trainers in affiliation with Extreme Execution, a service provided by Thomas & Thomas Consulting, LLC. They offer the Flight Assessment, a proprietary tool of Dr. Eric Thomas based on psychologist Dr. William Marston's DISC theory work.

Examining our behavior tendencies gives us valuable insights into our unique and personalized coping mechanisms and responses to loss. This gives us a deeper understanding of our unique capabilities (or strengths) and challenges (or limitations) in navigating self-awareness and being authentic. We can also use it in the grief journey, I do.

Understanding our Flight Assessment behavior types can allow us to recognize that each of us has a distinct way of processing grief. Some of us may lean toward action-oriented responses, seeking to address our emotions through practical tasks or problem-solving. Others may find solace in reflection and introspection, preferring to process their feelings internally before taking any outward action. By embracing our individual behavioral preferences, we can identify strategies that resonate with us personally, facilitating our healing journey.

For those with decisive or dominant behavior styles characterized by assertiveness, confidence, and a results-oriented approach, grief may be experienced as a challenge to overcome. These individuals may find solace in taking action, seeking practical solutions, and focusing on the tasks at hand. However, they may also struggle to express their emotions openly, leading to feelings of isolation and loneliness.

Conversely, individuals with interactive or influencing behavior styles, known for their outgoing nature, enthusiasm, and empathy, may find comfort in seeking support from others and sharing their feelings openly. However, they may also be prone to fluctuations in mood and may struggle to maintain boundaries with well-meaning but intrusive friends and family members.

Those with stabilizing or steady behavior styles, characterized by patience, empathy, and a calm demeanor, may find comfort in routines, ceremonies, and traditions. They may benefit from taking things one day at a time, focusing on self-care, and seeking support from trusted friends and family members. However, they may also struggle with change and may find it challenging to express their emotions openly.

Finally, individuals with cautious or conscientious behavior styles, known for their analytical nature, attention to detail, and desire for accuracy, may find solace in seeking answers, understanding the reasons behind their grief, and finding meaning in their loss. However, they may also be prone to overthinking and may struggle to let go of feelings of guilt or regret.

By recognizing our unique behavioral preferences and understanding how they influence our grief process, we can go through the loss journey with greater self-awareness, compassion, and resilience. (See the Appendix for more insight into how to use this information). Through self-reflection, support from others, and a commitment to healing, we can honor the memory of children and find meaning amid our pain.

Simple Tips for Mourners

As you process the healing journey, let the authors' grief experiences support you. They were gentle with themselves, recognizing the vulnerability of their hearts in the wake of their children's sudden departures. They found support in unexpected places—whether through the comforting words of clergy or the compassionate guidance of professional therapists. They honored their loved ones through their words and this collaborative effort, indicating their enduring bond with their children.

It's important to note that at the time of publishing this book, each of the authors had experienced the loss of their children within the last three years.

My loss was the most recent - being within the previous six months of the start of this book's draft. The wounds were still fresh, the pain still tender. Many nights, we spent in tears as we navigated the writing process; we were not crying because of the writing but because of the topic. It was painful, but it was necessary.

Yet, within our griefs, we found solace in community and a shared cause. This book was born from our united desire to offer hope—to shine a light in the shadows and remind others that they are not alone.

With resolve and a proactive mindset, we said, “Even though it's hard, we'll eventually get through it, and we'll be stronger, smarter, and tougher because of it.” And you will, too, after reading this.

Brigitte Jackson – Ubuntu Press, Editor-in-chief

THE UNWANTED CALL

The phone rang insistently, but I was deep in a business call and let it go to voicemail. It rang again, urgent, and persistent. I ended my current Zoom conversation with a prospective client. Sensing the urgency of my daughter's multiple missed calls, I saw that I had missed numerous calls from several people, even my ex-husband. I immediately called my daughter back. "Mom, is it true? Is it true!" Her words were frantic, repeating in a panicked loop. "Mom, is it true? Is it true!"

"Is what true?" I asked, my heart beginning to race with unease. She blurted out, "They said Jesse was killed. Mom, is it true?" I had no clue as to what she was talking about. It was as if she was speaking in a foreign language. At that moment, I realized that was why I had so many unknown phone numbers on my caller ID. As her words sank in, I ended the call and rushed downstairs to my husband.

"It's about Jesse," I gasped. Dread seized my chest as the unthinkable took shape in my words, as I slowly uttered. "Jesse has been found dead."

Desperate for answers, I began returning the missed calls, one belonging to my children's cousin who had been at the scene. The police officer was with her, and as I bombarded her with questions, she handed him the phone. In my anguish, I must have asked him a gazillion times—how did he identify my son? How could he be sure it was him? I wanted to know. He had to be mistaken, there was no way my son was gone. Each repetition was a plea for reassurance, a desperate attempt to grasp the unfathomable truth.

In the grip of an uncontainable surge of agony, I found myself outside, screaming into the sky, eventually ending up on my neighbor's porch. Stunned, I staggered back inside, grappling with the weight of the news that had blindsided me. Reality crashed down like a tidal wave, leaving me paralyzed in the dining room, standing like a deer in headlights.

The immobility turned to internal questioning. Just four hours prior, I was out in downtown Detroit passing out flyers by myself, attempting to help a mother from another state I did not even know find her missing adult child. How could this be happening to me? How? I had spent the day helping a stranger. I had stopped my busy workday to act in the ministry of love. All because the mom did not know anyone here in the area. How, God? How? While I was helping, my son was lying dead for who knows how many hours.

But before we go deeper into the ominous day of September 15, 2023, let's go back to September 1990; let me set the stage for the backdrop of my thinking and the heart-wrenching events that transpired before my son's demise.

Why So Much Pain

Have you ever muttered, or perhaps shouted, "This is the worst thing ever"? In my earlier years, I thought I knew hardship. But life had more to teach me as I grew older, revealing layers of anguish I could never have fathomed. I was in for many years of eye-opening experiences with grief and loss.

One of the most devastating experiences I had in my twenties was receiving the shocking news that my 18-year-old cousin had passed away. I was just 23, and the shock was so profound that I can barely recall who even told me the details. I was at Notre Dame University in Indiana with a group of college peers, attending a trip for a black think tank. The news abruptly shattered the excitement of being surrounded by brilliant minds and engaging in intellectually stimulating discussions. I spent the entire bus ride home full of joyful memories of the trip, which was soon tainted by overwhelming grief that would consume me when I arrived back in Flint, Michigan, and got off the charter bus in the University of Michigan parking lot.

For my maternal family, this loss marked the first death in over two decades. The last had been in 1970 when my Aunt Ella Mae, my mother's sister, and the eldest sibling, passed away. The circumstances of my cousin's death were the second most violent in our family's history, the first being the assassination of my uncle, Black Panther Mark Clark, in 1969 in Chicago, Illinois, when I was just three years old. While I have no personal memory of that event, its impact on my family was profound, with my grandmother fighting tirelessly for truth and justice. Years later, the civil court trial brought some semblance of closure, as the truth prevailed over the initial justifiable homicide ruling against the FBI, CPD, and Illinois State's Attorney's Office. Finally, my grandmother saw vindication in the courtroom.

But the pain of senseless murder did not end there. In 1990, tragedy struck again when my first cousin, Justin Clark, was senselessly gunned down in his driveway for intervening in a petty argument between his best friend and a young man in the neighborhood. Justin, with his gentle and compassionate nature, agonizingly bled out before medical help could arrive. His untimely death left a void that echoed with questions of senselessness and injustice. I cried for months, grappling with the unfathomable cruelty of his fate, questioning the fairness of a world where such a loving soul could meet such a violent end.

When my twenty-six-year-old sister was killed in a car accident seven years after my cousin's death, it felt like my insides would explode. I was eight months pregnant with my son Jesse at the time, the weight of grief compounded by the anticipation of new life. Over time, I managed to navigate through the grief, but the absence of my sister remained a profound ache.

Then, in 2001, four years after my sister's passing, three days before 911, my 32-year-old brother tragically died on my sister's birthday, struck by a hit-and-run driver. The flood of pain and agony returned with relentless force, overwhelming my soul once more. The pain I endured from losing loved ones deepened with each passing tragedy. Between 1997 and 2018, I also mourned the passing of the woman who helped define my Christianity: my maternal grandmother, Fannie Clark, and my paternal grandparents, Joe Barlow, Sallie Barlow, and Fannie Davis. Their absence further deepened the void in my heart–no more grandparents. Just like that, I was "grandparentless."

But nothing prepared me for the devastating loss of my father.

His death felt like a piece of my very being was torn away. The pain was so intense that there were days I curled up in bed in a fetal position, wishing I could disappear into the mattress and escape the torture of grief. My dad was not sick; I had no warning, only the precious thought that we were able to have a 37-minute conversation just hours before he closed his eyes and never woke back up.

Each successive loss seemed to prepare me for the unimaginable blow that would take my breath away—the loss that would become the defining moment of genuine grief. The grief I assume my grandmother felt losing two children within a year apart. Or my mom and dad felt like losing children. My mind could never ponder this type of grief, even after losing so many relatives over the years. Honestly, I had told God I had enough death before my dad's passing when I lost twenty-four loved ones in eight years. They stung in their own way, but when your child is taken, that is a different kind of grief.

Unlike before, when news of a loved one's passing left me silent with shock, praising God with my hands up, this time, I found myself running out of the house, screaming in raw despair. My cries echoed through the neighborhood, captured by surveillance cameras, leaving concerned neighbors checking in with each other to ensure I was okay.

NO, NOT MY SON

My mind struggled to grasp the reality of it all. I paced back and forth, unable to settle. My husband, noticing my restlessness, asked if I planned to drive to the scene and speak with the police in person. I replied with a hollow "no," leaving him puzzled by my reluctance. Despite my hesitancy for reality and the distance—

over 70 miles and at least an hour and a half drive—we found ourselves in the car, careering down the highway.

As we drove, our phones erupted with calls. My business line, personal phone, and my husband's device all clamored for attention, a level of concern, and inquiries. Amidst this flurry, a mentor called to have prayer with us, and together, we sought solace while navigating the congested, orange-tinted highway, the lanes constricting as if to mirror my fraying composure.

During that tense drive, doubt and disbelief battled within me. Was this nightmare absolute? As I continued to ponder, I recalled how I had interrogated the officer repeatedly over the phone, desperate for confirmation. Each time, his response echoed the same haunting truth—yes, it was him. Yes, this was real. Amidst the overwhelming emotions, I sought solace in music. I turned the radio up as loud as it could go and played "Stand" by Donnie McClurkin, allowing the lyrics to wash over me like a comforting embrace.

> *"Tell me, what do you give when you've given your all*
> *And it seems like you can't make it through.*
> *Well, you just stand when there's nothing left to do*
> *You just stand, watch the Lord see you through*
> *Yes, after you've done all you can*
> *You just stand"*

In my despair, I found strength in these words, a reminder to persevere even when faced with unimaginable pain. As I navigated the darkness, I clung to the belief that standing firm in faith would carry me through this storm of grief and uncertainty.

Finally arriving at the scene, the apartment complex was swarmed with police and onlookers, the street choked with vehicles. My legs carried me out of the car, unsteady but determined. I approached the detectives, mustering every ounce of strength to ask again the agonizing question: was it indeed my son? Their affirmative answer shattered me.

"I want to see him," I pleaded, but it was futile. The bodies had been taken by the medical examiner, leaving me empty-handed and yearning for closure.

In a haze of disbelief, I sought semblances of normalcy, attempting to comprehend the details the officers provided. Their theory—that my son had taken his own life—felt inconceivable to me. From the outset, I refused to accept it. Months have passed since that tragic day, yet I persist in pressing the police for answers. I adamantly maintained that someone else was involved and that my son's life was taken. The investigation remains active, and I will keep fighting for the truth. My prayers are intertwined with the book of Isaiah's plea for truth and justice from God, which is also my daily thought.

> *Isaiah 42:16 And I will bring the blind by a* **way** *that they knew not; I will lead them in paths that they have not known: I will make darkness light before them, and* **crooked** *things* **straight**. *These things will I do unto them, and not forsake them.*

The raw and profound experience of losing a child is a journey marked by tumultuous emotions, shattered dreams, and an enduring ache that echoes through the depths of the soul—compound that with the mystery of death, which is a parent's worst nightmare. There is no proper closure.

This was physiological – I felt like my heart was breaking into two pieces. Losing Jesse was not just losing a son; it was bidding farewell to a future intertwined with his laughter, his dreams, and his boundless love.

The Battle Between the Rational and Traumatized

Some days, I find myself uplifted, buoyed by a deep sense of worship, accompanied by grief and mourning. It explains the profound truth that God fearfully and wonderfully designed us, permeating us with remarkable abilities and internal strength beyond comprehension. Reflecting on the trauma of losing my son, my rational mind grapples with the enormity of the pain—questions swirl, doubts creep in, and a deep ache settles in my heart.

"Why did my son have to die that way, Lord? He loved you. He was a sweet young man, never touched by drugs or alcohol, never wandering the streets, or even fighting others. He was sheltered, growing up in a middle-class environment and a faith-based, church-going household. In his final week, he was outside, sharing cupcakes with a few neighborhood children. Why, my son? Why?" Despite the traditional cautions that questioning God is taboo, these questions echoed in my mind.

As an ordained minister, I am grounded in the belief that God is sovereign and loving and that His vision extends beyond the present moment. I remind myself that God sees all—the good and the evil—and that He knows the truth, even when it remains hidden from us. During my grief, I struggle to reconcile the unfathomable loss with my faith in a higher purpose.

The rational minister within me asserts that there will be no more hospitalizations, no more striving for a 'semblance of normalcy' that he viewed others enjoyed. Instead, I find solace in surrendering to God's sovereignty, trusting that His plan, though beyond my comprehension, will ultimately unfold for the greater good.

Though these questions persist in my heart, I acknowledge them as part of my journey—a journey marked by raw emotions, unyielding faith, and the courage to confront life's most profound mysteries. As I navigate this terrain of grief and uncertainty, I hold onto the belief that, in time, everything will find its resolution. I release the "what ifs" burden, allowing faith to guide me. Onward and forward.

Psalm 46:10 tells us to: Be still, and know that I am God; I will be exalted among the nations, I will be exalted in the earth. This scripture encourages us to find peace amid turmoil by trusting God's sovereignty and acknowledging His presence. It reminds us to release our burdens and anxieties to Him, allowing His guidance and wisdom to lead us on our journey.

In sharing my story, I offer a glimpse into the complex interplay between grief and faith, inviting others to find comfort in their struggles. Together, we navigate the depths of sorrow, finding strength in the shared journey of questioning, seeking, and ultimately, trusting in the unfailing love of our Creator.

Throughout Jesse's life, my husband and I served not only as parents but also as his guardians, protecting him through the challenges of living with a mental illness for the last twelve years of his life. Never did I imagine that we would lose him to death—that I would be unable to shield him from this ultimate fate.

My mind retreats to a place where he still exists, unable to fully accept the reality of his permanent absence at times. My imagination plays tricks on me because he was so woven into my regular routines that it is hard some days to realize it is just my brain trying to protect me, so it offers the vividness of his presence in my memories. He is gone. There are fleeting moments of sweetness, where memories bring comfort, followed by waves of anger and despair when I realize I can no longer touch him, hold him, or hear his voice.

My mood was unpredictable in the first few months, swinging between moments of calm reflection and overwhelming sorrow. It has been less than a year since Jesse's passing, and I am still immersed in the newness of this grief—a landscape marked by uncharted territory and unpredictable emotional terrain. Despite my pain, I find relief in encouraging others on their healing journeys. This echoes Jesse's spirit—he always gave despite his struggles. Even during hospital stays, Jesse would find ways to support and uplift those around him, embodying a resilience and compassion that inspires me.

As I navigate this tangled web of grief, I am reminded of Jesse's unwavering spirit and capacity to bring light into the lives of others. His legacy of kindness and empathy lives on in the hearts of those he touched. As I continue to heal, I am committed to honoring his memory by extending the same love and support to others who walk this path of loss and longing. Myles Munroe once said, "If your vision dies with you, you failed." Jesse surely did not fail because he was the epitome of love and kindness, so much so that phone calls continued to come in as they said, "Jesse would have done this." They are referring to him checking in on others.

The Worker Bee

Jesse, my beloved and tender-hearted boy, was the beating heart of our family—a unifying force that transcended generations. This truth became starkly evident at his standing-room-only funeral, where over 600 faces from across the country came to pay their respects over two days.

Reflecting on Jesse's relatively short life, I am reminded of the profound parallels between his journey and a worker bee's intense, purpose-driven activity within its finite lifespan. Just as the worker bee diligently gathers nectar and pollen to sustain its colony in its short weeks to months of life, Jesse's impact was similarly concentrated and far-reaching. He brought people together who had not spoken to each other in years, effortlessly restoring broken relationships.

The metaphor of the worker bee's short lifespan underscores the preciousness of time and the imperative of making every moment count. Jesse was keenly aware of life's fleeting nature, cherishing each experience and relationship with unwavering dedication. His urgency to make a positive impact was unmistakable, inspiring those around him to embrace life with similar passion and purpose.

Like the worker bee that pollinates thousands of flowers, Jesse's actions reverberated throughout our family and into the community, touching hearts and minds long after his passing. His ability to restore relationships and bridge divides exemplified a life lived with purpose—a testament to the profound impact that focused effort can have within a finite timeframe.

Contemplating the worker bee's short but impactful life prompts reflection on life's transient nature and the deep appreciation it cultivates. Jesse's journey taught me to cherish every moment, to seek beauty in life's complexities, and to forge meaningful connections that surpass time.

Jesse's life mirrored the essence of a worker bee—a life marked by intense dedication, purpose-driven actions, and a profound appreciation for the gift of each day. Though his time with us was cut short, his legacy continues to inspire and uplift us, reminding us of the significance of our contributions, regardless of the length of our journey.

As I continue to navigate the depths of grief and seek solace in faith, I extend this perspective to those burdened by the weight of loss. Our journeys are deeply personal, yet the common thread of profound love and enduring impact binds us together. Let us cherish every moment and embrace each day with purpose and intention.

My heart aches for those experiencing loss, especially if you are burdened by unanswered questions and shattered dreams like I was. I believe all things will eventually align for good despite the bleakness of loss. Not that the circumstances are good—there is nothing innately desirable about burying a beloved 26-year-old son, taken by a gun he abhorred. But within this tragedy, there is solace in the embrace of our God—our comforter, our guide.

May you find strength and solace in knowing you are not alone on this journey. Let us lean into the arms of faith, finding the courage to navigate the depths of our sorrow with hearts anchored in hope. In the silence of our prayers and the shared moments of remembrance, may we discover the transformative power of grace, weaving healing threads into the fabric of our brokenness.

Let us honor our beloved ones by carrying forward their legacy of love and impact, knowing that their light continues to shine brightly in the hearts of those they touched.

Tap Into Your Grief Cadence

We all have a cadence to our lives, unique and varied, often illuminated by the light of others around us. There will be sad days—inevitable, sporadic, and sometimes unexpectedly intense. It has been 27 years since my sister's passing and 23 years since my brother's, yet some days, it feels as though it happened only yesterday.

We each grieve differently, and we must honor our personal processes and ensure they are healthy and sustainable. As a coach and consultant specializing in behavior tendencies and emotional intelligence (EQ), I recognize emotional well-being's vital role in navigating the aftermath of loss.

In my profession, I understand the importance of self-awareness and coping mechanisms. Just as personalities shape our daily interactions, they also influence our grief journeys. I became my first client four years ago because I started coaching others. Putting in all that work allowed me to reap the benefits during my recent grieving process. I had an uncanny sense of awareness that supported me when my irrational brain kicked in.

As a behavior wealth strategist, I offer these reflections not as clinical advice but as personal insights into how taking the Flight Assessment, referenced in this book's introduction, can help you gain better self-awareness.

If you resonate with the decisive style, you may find solace in taking decisive actions, directing your grief into purposeful endeavors or advocacy work. Like me, those with an interactive style might seek comfort in social connections, sharing stories and memories with loved ones, and finding strength in community support. Stabilizing personalities thrive on stability and routine, so embrace practices that offer comfort, whether daily prayers, meditation, or time in nature. For the cautious types, seeking understanding and knowledge can be therapeutic. Dive into books, research, or support groups to navigate the complexities of grief.

While these suggestions are offered from a personal development perspective, I encourage seeking the guidance of licensed professionals for comprehensive, holistic support. May you find peace and resilience as you navigate this profound healing journey.

Brigitte Brown Jackson, Ed.S, is a distinguished behavior wealth strategist and the visionary founder of Exponential EduVentures, boasting 30 years of leadership experience, including 17 years at the helm of several charter schools. Brigitte's leadership style—driven by purpose, faith, and wisdom—has profoundly impacted audiences nationwide. Her passion for empowering teams shines through as she guides and inspires nationally, significantly influencing six- and seven-figure business owners by breaking barriers and shattering complacency.

A prolific best-selling author of seven books, Brigitte's insights and experiences offer invaluable guidance to many. A graduate of the University of Michigan (BS), Eastern Michigan University (MA), and Wayne State University (Ed.S) , she has also served as a teacher and principal, demonstrating her unwavering commitment to education and leadership.

As the founder of Kingdom Influence Global Ministry, Brigitte seamlessly blends her roles as a minister, wife, mother, grandmother, leader, and entrepreneur. She fosters positive change in individuals and organizations alike. Her presence is a beacon of hope, inspiring countless leaders to achieve their fullest potential.

For more information about Brigitte visit: www.brigittebrownjackson.com

"The value of life is not in its duration but in its donation. You are not important because of how long you live; you are important because of how effectively you live. Most people are concerned about growing old rather than being effective."

-Myles Munroe

#AFATHERSWORSTFEAR

Tragedy has a way of bookmarking itself in the hard drive of our minds. It's different for every person that experiences it. Not only is the traumatic event bookmarked, but the location finder is also enabled, kind of like a bad news GPS.

I bet you know exactly where you were and what you did when you received news about a horrific event. In my personal "history folder,"- I was in the high school library with my friends and a teacher when the space shuttle Challenger blew up before our eyes on national television. I was in the day room of my military dorm at R.A.F. Bentwaters in England, watching CNN as the Gulf War began and our squadrons began to deploy. My father, sister, and I sat in a conference room in South Sacramento, listening to one of the nation's top 5 cardiothoracic surgeons explain that I needed a second open heart surgery to correct the damage caused by the recent trauma of being stabbed or my heart would randomly explode. Snooks and I were in the bedroom of our first home, getting ready for work, when the news announced terrorists had attacked the Twin Towers. And the most traumatic of all, I was sitting at my home office desk when I saw my brother and sister-in-law pull up, unexpectedly, to the front of our house in their Toyota truck on June 22, 2023.

My wife's brother, a detective for the Sheriff's department, and his wife walked in when I opened the door, and I didn't notice the sullen look on their faces when I went to greet him with a hug. I made a couple of jokes, and he tried to smile, but his demeanor was uneasy. He said, "Bro, I have some news about Kaelin, and it's not good." Our son had some legal challenges in the past, so I asked if he was in jail again. He continued, "There was a call that came in about a shooting. It was Kaelin, and he didn't make it."

Wait! What?!

At that moment, I refused to believe it was my son. Did they fingerprint? Did he have an ID? Dental records? Could it be a case of mistaken identity? I challenged my brother, got on the phone with the medical examiner, and challenged her. I demanded to see the body, but it was an active investigation, and we weren't allowed access based on their protocol. I was lost, angry, confused, and believed that God had failed me.

I prayed many times for God to watch over our son as he struggled over the years. I would place him on the proverbial altar, tell God that Kaelin was his son before he was mine, and please deliver him. Of course, when I didn't see the progress I desired, I would intervene with my own solutions and practically take him back off the altar. But lately, Kaelin was different. He accepted responsibility for his actions. We had sober and revealing conversations. Something was different. My hope had returned. Only to learn that there was an altercation or disagreement between our son and some person. Kaelin wasn't known for backing down, but this one time, he turned to walk away and was shot multiple times by a still unknown assailant.

Have you ever felt like a breakthrough was right around the corner, but all you found was further disappointment? Why would God restore my hope only to rip it away along with my heart? I needed answers, and all I heard was silence. In the deep of night, when my soul ached, and everyone was asleep, I would scream into my pillow so I didn't awaken or scare anyone.

The following are excerpts from the real-time social media posts I shared during my emotional journey.

June 24, 2023 -

> Unfortunately, sorrow now has a permanent seat at our family table. Our hearts are heavy, our faith tested, and our hope stolen. Our son, Kaelin Cason, was murdered on Thursday, June 22nd, in South Sacramento. The proliferation of gun violence has to stop. We thank everyone who has been a source of light and inspiration in his life. Please hug your children no matter how old or what their plight in life may be. Tomorrow is not promised.

June 27, 2023 -

> I see ghosts of Kaelin everywhere. Driving into our court, I see a hint of him playing basketball. I hear a whisper of his goofy laugh as he watches Japanese anime in the living room. I can see his shadow rifling through the pantry, eating everything in sight. And I feel our last embrace on July 22, 2022, when he left our home for the final time. DO NOT TAKE YOUR CHILDREN FOR GRANTED. You can't assume they'll walk through the door again.

June 28, 2023 AM -

> I have buried my mother, my father, and my maternal and paternal sets of grandparents, and I thought I knew loss. Yes, I've longed to have one more conversation with my parents, but that

feeling pales in comparison to wanting to embrace, kiss, and give your own life for your child. Multiply the pain of losing parents and grandparents by 20, and you are scratching the surface of the pain of burying your child. Today, we had to meet with the funeral home. Though the staff was nice and professional, I wanted to leave immediately upon our arrival. "No words" is sincerely recited quite often by friends in reference to what we are going through. I've said it, too, when friends have experienced this torture, and I sought to console them. Words have not been created to describe the "falling into a deep well of despair" that is now our reality. I write because I hurt and need catharsis. I won't do this much longer because the cathartic effect of the moment ends as soon as I press next, and the profound loss of my son continues.

June 28, 2023 PM -

It hasn't been a week yet, and I'm writing my son's obituary. I can't think of a greater insult to the unalienable rights referenced in the Declaration of Independence. That part about Life, Liberty, and the pursuit of Happiness. It goes on to say that it's the right of the people to alter or abolish government (I say laws) that infringe on one's safety and happiness. The greatest infringement upon my son's (and our) right to live is the cavalier manner in which our nation embraces and distorts the 2nd amendment of the Constitution. I am a gun-owning war veteran who dedicated a portion of my life to the protection of our concept of democracy and the laws that support it. However, the National Safety Council states that "Suicide deaths involving guns have increased 28%, while assault deaths have increased 80% since 2012. In 2021, both suicide and assault deaths increased 8%." I lost my godson (little cousin) to suicide by gun in 2018 and my son last week to homicide (active investigation), so these aren't just statistics; they are my haunting reality. I pledged allegiance to "...the Republic for which it stands," and the republic is dying a very public and horrific death in our schools, in our homes, and in our streets. I support the 2nd Amendment AND our unalienable right to alter its governance to be more reflective of the protections guaranteed for the Republic's safety and well-being because we are far from ok. A torch isn't usually picked up until the fire touches your family; unfortunately, my home is ablaze. I make no appeal to the Democrats or, the Republicans or any political group. I'm pleading with our One Nation Under God to recognize that our amendments can be amended, but our dying children cannot be "undeathed". Consider having discussions in forums that will protect our republic because what we're doing isn't working. If this resonates with you in any way, positively or negatively, share it on your page to start a constructive conversation.

June 29, 2023 -

This past week has felt like an eternity of sorrow, pain, anger, loneliness, feeling lost, drunkenness, sadness, disbelief, and rage. There have been fleeting moments of reminiscent Black Boy Joy as strangers, friends, and family share stories, pictures, and videos of Kaelin. The support has been tremendous, and I know that our family will eventually rise above the melancholy funk we wake to every morning. Our first thought is of Kaelin, asking the universe if this is real. Is he really gone?! He wasn't here in the past, but he was always present. We answered every call, even the telemarketers because it could possibly be Kaelin. We lived expectantly with the hope of something better around the corner for him and his three beautiful children. Hope doesn't live here anymore. Every day this past week, my dark wolf has been nourished, slowly getting stronger. My wolf of light has also been encouraged and nourished, but the darkness that was buried in the basement is now in the yard. I haven't seen or fed him in decades, but he lurks, waits, and looks for something or someone to devour. This is my authentic truth. My reality. My pain. One week ago, we were at a doctor's appointment with our grandson, three exits from where our son was being murdered at the exact same time. There were no premonitions, intuitions, or supernatural manifestations. The notice came hours later. And the other wolf was awakened. I'm fully aware that the one you feed is the one that grows. We pleaded with my son to feed the wolf of light, and when he finally did, his life was taken. And so my dark wolf is hungry, angry, in the shadows, and ever-present, but I believe it's protecting the light and ready to pounce on any darkness that encroaches on my family's light. Or it's taking over. I'm not quite sure yet.

June 30, 2023 -

The Asterisk* - Snooks said something today that stopped me in my tracks. She said that our lives now have an asterisk attached to it. Everything we've done or will do after June 22, 2023, has the asterisk of *post-Kaelin". It doesn't mean we won't smile, travel, love, dance, or create new milestones. It means I can now describe that empty feeling sitting in the center of my soul. It doesn't detract from my immense love for Snooks, Ashanti, Keauna, or the Grands. It just gives me a visual representation of what is indescribable.

June Reflection: *There are no words to describe the immense feeling of loss, anger, resentment, guilt, and anxiety. My faith was shaken to its core. God gave us so many signs that our son was on the mend, and we both had a new sense of hope that brighter days were ahead. And then the clouds gathered, and the storm began.*

July 3, 2023 -

This is exhausting. I've already mentioned the emotional rollercoaster we're all on, and it's never in sync. I'm up, she's down. The girls are up and console us when we're down. We're all down and in separate rooms to not cause mass hysteria and scare the Grands. Now stack the preparations for Kaelin's service on top of it all, and we're reviewing pictures and videos and baiting grief at every turn. Smiling one second and wiping tears the next. All griefs aren't built the same. I've grieved my mother, and it was hard. I've grieved my father, and that was hard, too. I've also grieved all my grandparents. They were all melancholy, and tears were shed. Grieving a child who was murdered, raising his son, and having no answers to satiate the "whys" racing through your mind is a special kind of hell I don't wish on anyone. I am not Job. I question the F@&# out of God, and He doesn't give me answers, but He does grant me peace (most times). Sometimes the rage is on ten and He just allows me to vent. There isn't anything anyone can do for us except pray for the sanity and unity of our family, and that the gift of discernment be granted to the law enforcement and prosecutors seeking justice on our behalf. Also, pray for your families and remove any barriers that may exist between you and your children. We are blessed to know that the last words exchanged between Kaelin, Ronna, and myself were positive affirmations and lots of love. Make sure your children have the same.

July 4, 2023 -

And the rollercoaster continues. I write because it's cathartic and it helps me. It's not meant to entertain or solicit sympathy. It's a release valve I use, so I don't explode. This morning, my oldest and dearest friends shared some pics of Kaelin for us to use, and the dam of emotions just crumbled, and so much came out. But I had to stifle my screams and rage because the children were here. If pillows could talk, the screams these have captured would be deafening. I reached out to them and shared "that the pain is hard to explain, but I miss him, and I miss the hope I carried every day for him to turn things around. I'm pissed at God because I absolutely trusted Him, and He gave me so many signs that trusting Him was right and that Kae was going to be alright eventually. I placed him on God's altar and said he was your son first. Please help him. I trusted God, and I feel betrayed. We've helped couples overcome betrayal and build bridges of trust again. I don't know how that's possible here. I don't hate God, but

I don't trust Him either." I had another interaction with someone else that I dearly love. She loves us every day and asks if we need anything. My response is usually prayer, but today, I said, "I need my son to come home. I need to know why God betrayed my trust. I need to know what the f@&# the police are doing to rip the heart out of the spineless MF who murdered our son. I need many things that can't be given, but I'll accept your love." And I'll continue to humbly accept your love and prayers for our family. We struggle daily and will for quite some time, but I doubt that I'll continue to journal in this manner for much longer. God and I will work it out like we always do. His patience is much more enduring than mine.

July 7, 2023 -

The sun has risen, yet darkness remains. A constant fog hangs relentlessly, even in the presence of light. Joys present themselves, and we embrace them, but even those moments are enveloped in despair. It's like a shadow of sorrow lurks around every corner waiting for the light to shift slightly so it can present itself. You might not see it now, but it's there. Waiting. Expectantly. Looking for the angles. Patiently biding its time until that photo, song, clothing, smell, memory, or gesture reminds you of him. And yet, we refuse to allow that second death. The one that comes if Kaelin's name is no longer mentioned, when stories stop being told, or the pain of his absence is avoided.

July 8, 2023 -

We take a lot of deep breaths around here. I mean "a lot, a lot" of deep breaths. It's become synonymous with "pause, gather yourself." Before talking with the Grands... a deep breath. Before answering the phone, I took a deep breath. Before responding to each other...deeeeep breath. While watching an episode of "I am Virgo" on Prime Video and, someone unexpectedly dies (no spoiler alert)...multiple deep breaths. So many things are triggering deep breaths. I even took one before starting this post.

When you see us in passing, or if you choose to text or call, I invite you to also take a deep breath before asking about the case, how we're doing, or sharing your thoughts on the situation. It hasn't happened often, but...deep breath.

July 11, 2023 -

What happens when your very first "Why" is suddenly stolen from you? Let's be honest. Many of you know the kinder, gentler version of me. When I was in the Air Force overseas, I was a jerk – a typical ugly American whose lifestyle involved drinking, fighting, and women (unmarried and married). I was young and messy. When I returned stateside, I wasn't much better, but my sphere of exposure began to change. Friends at Holloman A.F.B influenced me to begin a different path back toward who I was meant to be. And then my "Why" arrived. Kaelin Cason was the catalyst that changed everything in my life - spiritually, physically, and mentally. Our road was challenging, single father and son, and then Ronna (Snooks) accepted us into her life. And the road became more challenging. If you know our story...you know! But my why became Ronna's why, and then we added two more "Whys" to our crazy family. There were tribulations and triumphs, laughter, and tears, just like every other family. Our dysfunction was similar to many other families and different all at the same time, but we grew as a family and as human beings. Kaelin wasn't perfect, much like his father, and he had stuff to work through, also like his father and everyone else, but he is no longer with us physically. Much was left unresolved, but the "I Love You's and hope for redemption" were firmly in place. My first Why may be gone physically, but what he represented and still represents lives strongly within his sisters, his children, and the hopes and dreams he and I spoke about but never realized together. As long as I have breath, his story continues in me, his mom, sisters, and children. So, I guess my first "Why" is still right where it has always been ...in my heart!

July 13, 2023 -

I've read the phrase, "shell of my former self," in many books and thought it to be a great descriptor. Now, I personify the phrase. I used to think "imposter syndrome" was limited to being in social or professional "rooms" you found your way into but questioned the validity of your membership. Now, I wonder about my ability to protect, lead, and provide for my family. I look around and realize I've become the living patriarch of the family, and I've lost my only son. His murder is unsolved; I don't have room in my heart for vengeance, and I admit I'm lost. All I want to do is explode and scream, but I can't because I need to protect the frailty and innocence of Isaiah while creating space for my girls (Snooks, Ashanti, and Keauna) to grieve freely and openly. Being strong for them weakens my resolve to stand in the gap for others, and I'm exhausted. I've coached girls for a long time and tried to build their self-confidence. Snooks and I answered a shared calling and have built an impactful marriage coaching business. I've poured so much into others and couldn't rescue my own son. That makes me question my identity on every level. Was my focus misguided? Was I too stringent? Too lenient? Distracted? Am I overly focused, now, on who I've lost versus who remains in front of me? So many questions and so few answers. Friday and Saturday will, arguably, be the most difficult days of my life. I thank everyone for your prayers and support, but I also ask for your grace in advance. I don't know how I'll show up for the next 48 - 72 hours or the rest of my life, but I do know it will be different from when Kaelin was alive. The air of confidence, belief, expectation, and hope is musty with a tinge of sorrow, despair, anxiety, and anger. Forgive me in advance, hence the grace. I am not the same.

July 15, 2023 -

I guess I'm "Doubting Thomas." I've been working through grief on the assumption that what I've been told is true. We saw our son tonight for the first (and last) time since his murder. Some things aren't truly real until you see them. Seeing our son was confirmation the nightmare is real. Confirmation our love is real and enduring. Confirmation that things will never be the same. Confirmation that our family is forever changed. It was gut-wrenching, visceral, and a necessary part of our healing process. Though it was my last glimpse of him, it isn't my lasting memory of him. Peace, Shalom, One Love, my dearest son.

July 15, 2023 -

No one should ever see their child in a casket. It's unnatural, and you can't unsee it. The vision sears itself into your consciousness on multiple levels. The mental slideshow that is our memory now has this rebound effect where I see him playing basketball, then casket. Harassing his sisters, casket. Hugging his mom casket. And so forth. Yesterday was necessary, but it was also haunting. I previously mentioned that I felt like a shell of my former self. I stand corrected after viewing the shell of what was my son. His shell was in the casket, but his life was in the room. His mom, sisters, aunts, uncles, cousins, grandparents, friends, and associates who shared memories, cried, laughed, told stories, and offered love to each other are his true testament to existence. I'll struggle for a while with this casket vision, but the love in that room and later today at his Celebration of Life will go a long way toward my healing. Everlasting Love for my boy.

July 18, 2023 -

Snooks and I are damn good at helping others through difficult times. Why are we struggling to do the same for ourselves? Nothing can prepare you for this. It's a fractured reality that shifts without notice. One minute, you are focused on a task, and then you're staring off in the distance at nothing at all, wondering what you were doing. It takes a moment, then you remember, but now you want to cry because...well, just because. Anger, sadness, "meh-ness," and an occasional smile or laugh battle under the iceberg for the right to break the surface. I've been trying to work out for the last 5 hours, and when I finally start the music, the first lyrics I hear are "It's ok to not be ok" (by Derek Minor). So, I'm crying again. The only thing getting a workout are my emotions and tear ducts. Again, I write for me. If this is too dark or melancholy, just scroll and enjoy your blessings. I plan to post about Kaelin's Celebration of Life, but when I view the beautiful celebration pics and videos, the workout begins again. Keep us in prayer because I have to find a functional balance at some point.

July 20, 2023 AM -

Everything is so grayed out. All the things that gave me so much joy are just "meh" now, with the exception of the Girls and the Grands. They breathe color into my life. Ashanti and Keauna are everything to me and now I'm scared every time they leave the house. I make it a point to let them know they are loved before they go to the store, work, or out with friends. I'm trying not to take their presence for granted. I miss them dearly when they are gone. When they return, so does the color. They are safe. I no longer trust the world. I watched the first episode of "Sweet Tooth" on Netflix last night and completely identified with Pubba. His efforts to protect his child made sense to me. The world stole my son before he completed his transformation, so now trust is reserved strictly for immediate family, extended family adopted family, and work family. That's who came to celebrate my boy's life and that's who have my undying alliance. The rest of the world gets the side eye. When the girls and grands aren't around, I'm reduced from 31 Flavors to just vanilla.

July 20, 2023 PM -

I'm sitting at my computer scanning the expenses for Kaelin's Memorial, and it asks what I should call the file. "Funeral? Memorial? Celebration of Life? Or Death Expenses." That's literally what ran through my head. I lingered on the word "death." My son's death expenses. He is dead. Murdered. Shot in cold blood and his murder is actively being investigated, but unsolved. The

TEAR Model of Grief talks about: T= To accept the reality of loss, E= Experience the pain of the loss, A= Adjust to the new environment without the lost person, and R= Reinvest in the new reality. We are slowly progressing through this process. It isn't linear. It's a hopscotch of jumping from one to another and back to the last one and then over to another. It's nonstop. And my mind comes back to death. Died. Killed. Passed away. Murdered. No longer with us. That last one isn't exactly true. He is with us. I carry him with me moment by moment, minute by minute, hour by hour, day by day, as my Lord and Savior carries me. I don't have to look at the footprints in the sand because I know they aren't mine. Just like the burden of these TEARs; I don't carry them alone.

July 25, 2023 -

There's no sugarcoating it. Nights are extremely hard. The days are better (not easier, just better). Daylight creates an environment conducive to distractions. Friends, family, remodeling, yard work, grandchildren, etc. But when the grind begins to slow and people and tasks are being tucked in, I see Kaelin's photos. I'll see him in Isaiah's sleeping face, and in the game room, and in the living room, and in the recesses of my mind wondering why there aren't any answers regarding his murder. I've gone from being relatively healthy to needing anxiety medication, alcohol, and busy work. I thought I was having a heart attack 3x since his death and ended up in urgent care once. My facial skin and scalp are discolored, dry no matter how much I moisturize, and sleep is spotty at best. And the world keeps spinning. Everyone's lives, including ours, continue to move forward while K's stopped abruptly. And it doesn't feel right...mostly at night when his presence and absence are felt most.

July 27, 2023 -

I saw a statue on social media that spoke to me on so many levels.

It was of a man that was hollow and barely held together. It made me think about the meaning of life; not that life is meaningless, but the things that brought me joy or passion before aren't even registering now. I used to get an itch to coach volleyball around this time of year, but that sensation is gone. Our focus will be helping couples through adversity and dealing with the "hard things" we never knew we signed up for.

July 31, 2023 -

I whisked my family away from the valley to connect with ourselves and each other as we continue this unwanted journey of healing. We did some things alone and we did some things together. But in all that we did and do, we remain family. Rarely in the moment do I feel Kaelin's absence. It's the aftertaste of the moment when his particular flavor rises above others. It's the note that's not heard or won't ever be heard again that sobers me from being drunk on life. Kaelin wasn't present in many of our family adventures because he was doing his own thing, but that was his choice. Not being here now or ever again was a decision made by some faceless coward. Our family narrative has been forever altered and we are attempting to live as Bravvo did. Fearless, Unapologetic, Bold, Sometimes Right, Sometimes Wrong, but always Passionate. We got uncomfortable and did something we might never have done under normal circumstances. Kaelin, in his own way, inspires us all to live, love, laugh, and cry enough for both of us, so if you see one of us being quiet, shedding a tear, cooking feverishly, telling a joke, or whatever, just know we're doing it for ourselves and Kaelin simultaneously.

July Reflection: *I looked and felt like crap. I had multiple anxiety attacks for the first time in my life and had prescription medication prescribed to help me sleep. Hot Mess didn't begin to describe what I was, and yet I continued to lean on God even though I didn't like Him very much in the moment.*

August 4, 2023 -

(Listening to podcast) This is so eerie. It's like we did this interview (Married Into Crazy Podcast, episode 204) a year in advance to help us through the worst period of our lives. Yesterday was an odd day. It marked 6 weeks after Kaelin's murder; I picked up his ashes from the funeral home, and it was Isaiah's 4th Birthday. The phrase, "Smiling through the pain," doesn't begin to scratch the surface of what we've been doing around here. Yesterday and today feels like we lost him all over again (placed his death certificate in the same folder as his birth certificate), but we refuse to penalize Zay because of our sorrow. In protecting him, I fear we are stunting our healing process. I'm glad we did this podcast a year ago, but I also wish we didn't need to listen to it for guidance.

August 5, 2023 -

I love authenticity, but I have to confess we've been everything but authentic. The smile, the nod, the laughter.... It doesn't matter if it's personal or professional, it's a farce. 6 weeks later, I can't begin to describe the pain my family is still experiencing. This never ends. Just when you think the grief is subsiding, your breath, spirit, and joy are ripped from you again for no reason other than you are experiencing The Year of Firsts. What the f@$k am I going to do on Kaelin's birthday in December? We've gone from looking forward to milestones to dreading them. This isn't how we're supposed to live and this wasn't supposed to happen to my family. Ronna and I weren't charmed, but we were blessed. Both finishing school later in life, grinding, serving, blessing others, and now we're battling depression and I'm taking anxiety meds to avoid panic attacks. The last two days have been absolutely horrible. I see how families can collapse under the pressure of losing a child, no matter what the age. We aren't at the brink of collapsing, but we are so very tired. Sleep is elusive and the nightmare begins when the sun rises. We're authentically tired and just trying to make it day to day. Pardon the smile.

August 10, 2023 -

I broke down while on the treadmill this morning as I was thinking about the day's tasks. A wave of guilt, regret, and shame overcame me because I chastised myself for "moving on" as my son's ashes rested in an urn downstairs. It was like having a ton of bricks land on me. My watch indicated that my heart rate increased dramatically and I was on the verge of another panic attack. Seeing my heart rate gave me a chance to focus on reducing it by box breathing and coming to terms (in the moment) with choosing the light and focusing on "moving with" my son into the future and not necessarily "moving on."

August 17, 2023 -

This feeling of grief is prominent this morning and I assume it will continue to be as we experience all those "firsts" in Kaelin's absence. Isaiah starts his educational journey today with his very first day of school. Papa, Snooks (as he calls her), Ashanti, and Keauna will be his rocks in his father's absence and will power through to make it as wonderful as possible while each of us battle through this grief. Smiles on, upward, and onward!

August 27, 2023 -

There was victory in the air yesterday (and we aren't done). What could have been a potentially devastating day was glorious. We cleared out a lot of Kaelin's belongings including some furniture in order to make the room truly Isaiah's. We posted and gave furniture to a pair of random young couples beginning their parenting journeys and it felt good. Zay was excited to have a bright new space of his own. He mastered how to go up and down his ladder and was so proud of himself. More of Kaelin's clothes, some with tags still on them, will be donated this week to provide new starts for some young men in the community. I'm sure there are lessons in here somewhere, but we're just going to focus on Zay's smiles.

August Reflection: *This was a transitional month with so much to unpack. The year of "firsts" began and hurt something fierce. I lost count of how many times I screamed into a pillow or beat my steering wheel into submission while yelling at the top of my lungs about how unfair life is. A variation of Friedrich Nietzsche's quote played on repeat in my head, "Life is just and unjust, and justified in both." I hated that my subconscious was somehow trying to rationalize my son's murder.*

September Reflection: *I was in a very dark place and purposefully chose to refrain from posting anything regarding my son or what I was feeling. Probably not the healthiest thing to do, but it also didn't darken anyone else's days.*

October 8, 2023 -

In a moment of complete focus, I found the energy to sit and review my retirement portfolio and make adjustments based on some expert advice received back in May. Pretax, post tax, Roth catch up contribution adjustments, etc. and then the page came up re: beneficiaries and it listed our son, Kaelin, as deceased. I can't muster the strength to remove him from our records. It feels like betrayal. It doesn't seem right that one click could remove him from our financial family archive. I haven't been posting our daily struggles because I know it's our journey and people look for positive things on their timelines. So I post our distractions...speaking engagements, Vegas excursions, work trips, foodie crap, Isaiah's exploits, and the sort, but for every 1 post I promise there are 5-6 (if not more) breakdowns. I've led corporate meetings or participated in them via Zoom and cried and wailed in the breaks between. Snooks and I are not ok, but we lean on God and limp forward. Our son is not deceased; he was murdered, and it is still unsolved, and we remain in a state of unrest...with smiles on as we pose for the next picture.

October 27, 2023 -

(Praise Report - Not a complaint) I am not worthy, and yet God continues to bless me. (And He blesses you, too!) From being cut with a razor blade in high school to totaling my car on I-5 after falling asleep at the wheel, to being stabbed THROUGH the heart, two open heart surgeries, almost divorced, surviving bladder cancer, losing our firstborn to murder recently, to testing positive for TB but chest x-ray shows no signs... God has been with me the entire time. Even now, as a result of the TB test, additional blood panel testing, and a liver ultrasound...early signs of nonalcoholic fatty liver disease have been added to my life resume. Y'all, my Champion qualifications keep getting better and better. And for what?? To remind everyone that reads this that "If You're Breathin,' It's Your Season!" My son didn't miraculously awake this morning, but I did. So, it's my season to say his name aloud (Kaelin Cason) and tell his children stories about him. For whatever reason, God says it's my season to love my wife with all my heart and show my daughters what love and adoration look like so they know what to expect. It's my season to reverse this minor fatty liver disease through nutrition, exercise, and better choices. Yes, life can be hard, but those moments pale in comparison to the blessings God provides if we choose to see them. Sorrow still sits at my table, but I see that Joy, Love, Endurance, Forgiveness, Anger, and Happiness have also pulled up a seat. We break bread together and celebrate ALL that God brings us daily. After all, It's Our Season.

October Reflection: *I yelled less at God and surrendered to Him. I was not close to being healed and not sure I ever will be, but I did remove the blame from God. I can't say I was at peace, but it wasn't as foreign as it had been in recent months.*

November 30, 2023 -

This grief struggle is REAL! I saw a homeless person yesterday and after I turned my head, Kaelin's face was seared on the person I saw, and I still see him when I close my eyes. Today the lead detective called to ask if they can reach out to the public for help again because all leads have dried up. Kaelin's birthday is this Sunday, and though he should be turning 29, he will be Forever 28. I referred to Isaiah multiple times today as Kaelin. There's this constant battle between my logical and emotional sides, and I just get angry. Yes, "Give yourself grace. It takes time. Feel what you feel. Etc." I know. It just sucks in ways I can never articulate. Writing is cathartic at times, so I cry, yell, laugh, reminisce, and continue to write some more. This is one of those things you don't know to write into your vows. We are strong together, but we are battered. Showing strength for our girls, Isaiah, and our granddaughters takes so much energy, there's little bandwidth for much else. They rise joyous and expectant, so we do, even if it's to live vicariously through their precious moments. Some grays are giving way to color again, but some grays are permanent, and that's what we're still coming to terms with, especially during this time of year. Yeah, this season's colors are red, green, and gray.

November Reflection: *I kept wanting to get back to normal and I realized that there was no "getting back" to anything. Everything had changed. I was being led to embrace the "new normal," which included a lot of discomfort, intermittent sorrow, and random triggers around every corner. But there were also new joys being found in the holiday dynamics with Isaiah (along with a lot of challenges).*

December 3, 2023

Happy Heavenly Birthday to my first born, the catalyst for all that I am. Nothing I can say or do will bring you back, but you are present in ALL that I do. I love and miss you desperately.

December 18, 2023 -

For the first time, in a long time, Kaelin is home for Christmas. And it hurts like a Mother£#}€r. He hasn't been present in many ways and now that he is (albeit in an urn), it just underscores all the opportunities we all missed out on. His children don't get to experience the Christmas Eve Hijinks, or argue with him about going to bed early, or take part in the 25 Days of Christmas movie parade so dear to Snooks. We just get our personalized version of Charles Dickens's " A Christmas Carol" with visions of Christmas Past on repeat because no future includes our son. He was no angel or martyr that was above reproach, but was and is our son who lost his opportunity at redemption and reconciliation with his children. Tonight, a Mack Truck of grief ran me over when I least expected it, and all I could do was surrender in tears and submission. I was useless at the moment and checked out. The wind was blowing, and I could hear the wind chimes some anonymous doner sent in Kaelin's memory, but it wasn't enough. If Isaiah weren't here, I would be in a drunken stupor, but here I sit, drenched in tears...sober, and not happy about it. There's no escaping this new reality of hope without hope. Merry Christmas, indeed.

December 25, 2023 -

It was a fun and emotional morning. All of our Christmas traditions leading up to today have been "off," sporadic at best. But we created new traditions with Isaiah, like introducing Nix and his bag of tricks. We've had happiness, sadness, joy, and pain. We're not ok, but that's okay. We are growing in ways we never anticipated or knew we needed. After we opened all the presents, one remained. It was from Kaelin by way of Deborah Larson and the "Horses Healing Heroes" organization. This was Kaelin's happy place, his zen. This portrait of Kaelin with wings near a horse is a blessing, and I believe that he is watching over us, his children, and the ranch. Upon opening the gift, tears were shed, but smiles were present. Thank you, Deborah.

December 31, 2023 -

Have a Blessed, Happy, Transformative, and Healing New Year. I've heard people mention experiencing highs and lows, in passing, without much context. I began 2023 six months into the most challenging and amazing role of my medical sales career and traveled to Turks and Caicos with 16 additional family members. We had the BEST room in the entire resort (people stopped, gawked, and actually asked how we liked the room), had the time of our lives, and then came home to a nightmare that will reverberate through the rest of our lives. Our son was murdered 3 days after we returned home, and the case remains unsolved with no leads. Highs and lows don't begin to explain what we endured in 2023. While I am excited and committed to being the best version of myself in 2024 and beyond, I also dread facing a year that will not include my son's heartbeat or footprint in it. There are no words I can share or that anyone can lend that will calm the constant storm in my heart and mind. I personally know three other parents that lost their sons in 2023, and several more that lost sons over the years. It feels like a pandemic, and I have anxiety every time our daughters leave the house. Seriously. Anxiety medication and two different therapists have been part of my "self-care" in 2023. And yet, I don't want the year to end because my son had breath, hope, and an opportunity at reconciliation. None of that exists in the new year. All is not bleak, though. My mentor and friend, Dr. Eric Thomas, often talks about turning our pain into purpose, and there are some things in motion to do exactly that. 2024 will be a year of transformation and healing. In my book, that's a year worth looking forward to.

December Reflection: *Christmas was a struggle. We found ourselves trying to create new traditions for Isaiah (and for us). Everything we did was tempered with the knowledge that there was no hoping Kaelin would join us this year or ever again. The weather began to turn, and the winds picked up quite a bit. I mention this only because someone anonymously sent some wind chimes with a scripture written on them. Every time the wind blew, I imagined the chimes were Kaelin's new voice, and he was letting us know he was at peace and that we should be, too.*

Epilogue: New Year, New Me….

Well, not quite. It's more like different. My apprehension about the new year was real, but most of my anxiety was tethered to my attempts to get our family "back" to a normal that didn't exist. Unfortunately, gun violence has created a community of grieving parents, and I was blessed to be surrounded by both fathers and mothers who chose to channel their pain into purpose. Two fathers in my King's Accountability Group and several dads in my friend circle lost their sons before us and offered wise counsel.

Men need to cry, scream, and yell. Strength isn't demonstrated by holding in your emotions. It's displayed through the vulnerability of letting the world know how much you loved your child. I was advised to create a new normal because everything had changed, and trying to reclaim old norms would just invite frustration. I started, and continue, seeing a therapist weekly to help me process and navigate the anticipated waves of grief that accompany the "year of firsts" without my son.

Between my network of purposeful parents and my therapist, I learned the following tips:

1. **Respect your grief** and willingly give her a seat at the table when she arrives. It's not a matter of if she comes; it's when. It may happen at the most inopportune times but create a mindset that allows you a cathartic release when needed. The people that matter will understand and support you.
2. **Seek solitude**, not isolation. There is a difference. Solitude is sought for reflection, introspection, or personal growth. Isolation involves cutting yourself off from others, leading to loneliness and disconnection. Solitude can be a positive

and enriching experience, while isolation often has negative associations.

3. **Breathe!** In those moments when you are flooded, full of emotion, and your heart begins to race, try box breathing. Inhale for 4 seconds, hold your breath for 4 seconds, exhale for 4 seconds, and hold for 4 seconds. Inhale, hold, exhale, hold. Keep repeating until you are able to relax a little.

I leave you with this scripture: "The Lord is close to the brokenhearted and saves those who are crushed in spirit." Psalm 34:18

If you need another way to truly visualize it, consider The Message Bible version, which says, "If your heart is broken, you'll find God right there; if you're kicked in the gut, he'll help you catch your breath." I could not make it plainer.

Ernie "Lovey" Cason is an exceptional Marriage Mentor who, alongside his wife of over 27 years, co-hosts the widely acclaimed "Married Into Crazy®" podcast, renowned as one of the most impactful marriage podcasts globally. His extensive experience as a keynote speaker, TEDx speaker, marriage advocate, Couple 2 Couple Coach, author, dedicated husband, father, and proud Gulf War veteran enriches his ability to guide couples towards thriving relationships.

Ernie's approach draws from his Extreme Execution training and his certifications in Level 1 & 2 Gottman Method Couples Therapy. With a commitment to compassionate, real, accountable, zealous, and yielding (C.R.A.Z.Y.) methods, Ernie and his wife empower couples to overcome challenges and cultivate lasting and loving relationships.

Their dedication extends beyond their professional endeavors; Ernie and his wife are proud parents to one son, who they hold in their hearts forever at 28, two daughters, and three grandchildren. Through their platform, they serve marriages globally, offering support and guidance to couples seeking to strengthen their bonds.

For more information on Ernie's work and how he champions marriages worldwide, visit www.MarriedIntoCrazy.com.

.

"You have within you right now everything you need to deal with whatever the world can throw at you."

- Brian Tracy

MY JOURNEY FROM PAIN TO PURPOSE

Every day we wake up, there are times filled with hope, but they can quickly turn challenging. That was the case on March 14, 1982, when my journey into motherhood began. It was a significant occasion, filled with the warmth and tenderness of thoughts of embracing my newborn child for the first time. Arriving at the hospital, I was beyond overjoyed. I had asked God for this. Motherhood was my desire. However, as the day unfolded and the delivery was complete, I was faced with a plethora of unexpected complications.

After delivering my son, obstacles arose, and I found myself whisked away into the sterile confines of the operating room, leaving behind my precious new baby boy, and confronting the unknown. It was unbelievable; I was rushed to emergency surgery. There were hospital staff all around me. How could a day that emerged with the joy of motherhood swiftly give way to uncertainty and panic?

Most women who deliver spend time in the recovery room are at the highest moments of joy and delight. We didn't have birthing rooms back then like they do now. You were moved from room to room. During my convalescence and recovery time, it was quite the opposite; the doctor called my family to the hospital and said: "We don't expect Ruby to live. If she does survive this, she will have health complications and will not be able to have another child."

The doctor's solemn words reverberated in their minds —words of doubt and despair threatened to overshadow the beautiful moment of the new life that was brought into the family. But even in the darkest of hours, there remained a steadfast signal of faith—a conviction that God held us in His tender care, regardless of the news my family had been given.

Unaware of the gravity of my condition, I was in excruciating pain, lying in a hospital room, when a nurse quietly entered, her demeanor carrying an air of solemnity. With gentle but weighty words, she conveyed the news that my newly born son would be discharged into the care of his father, a decision that stirred confusion and apprehension within me. Despite my persistent questioning, answers remained confusing, compelling me to request the presence of my doctor urgently. When the doctor eventually arrived, I poured out my fears, articulating my distress at the thought of being separated from my son. Unaware of their intentions, they were preparing for me to remain in the hospital. I was oblivious to the fact that they were preparing for the worst—that I might not make it. My body was full of pain, which took a lot of my focus. All I was focused on was relief from this very uncomfortable situation I found myself in. I came to the hospital with the great expectation of delivering a healthy baby boy without complications to my body. What do you do when circumstances go the other way? I just kept crying out to God, asking Him for relief. I was not quoting scriptures and certainly was not decreeing and declaring the word of God.

Reflecting on that time, I am so grateful for my praying mother, who I now know was interceding along with the people of God on my behalf. There will come times in our lives when we cannot pray, but God will move on our behalf through the faith of others—believing men and women of God who will bombard heaven on our behalf. By which I am here today.

My former pastor and a couple of missionaries from my church visited me during my hospital stay. Their arrival seemed like a routine visit at first, but as they gathered around my bedside, I sensed their purpose was far more profound—they had come to intercede on my behalf through prayer. Nothing was going to get me through this, but God.

Miracles Do Exist

Each day, I sought comfort in conversations with my mother, confiding in her the depths of my suffering. Yet, in her wisdom, she shielded me from the harsh prognosis, offering words of reassurance and hope instead, a steadfast anchor in the post-delivery battle. The prayers of my visitors, coupled with my mother's unwavering faith, were indeed answered by the divine, evidenced by my continued presence.

The daily visits from my newborn son brought a glimmer of joy to my bedside, infusing me with renewed determination to persevere. Despite the confines of my bed, bound by the complications of surgery, the devoted presence of my fiancé, though anxious with his own fears, provided a steady source of comfort and support.

Despite the grim prediction of the medical staff that I had received, my hospital stay was only a month. Soon after, I was embarking on the journey to recovery outside of the confines of the hospital. Returning home, my mother gently told me of the stark reality of my situation, contrasting sharply with my hopeful expectations. Yet, within the gloomy news, a revelation emerged—I was not destined for the embrace of death but for the gift of life. God, in His infinite mercy, blessed me with the miracle of existence, a double grace presented in the form of my son and the continuation of my own life.

Reflecting on the chaotic chapters of my first birthing experience, I am reminded of faith's unwavering power, intercession's transformative effectiveness, and the enduring grace that lights our path through life's darkest valleys. Though veiled in uncertainty, our journey is guided by the radiant hand of God, leading us from the depths of despair to the triumphant dawn of a new day. In the trials and triumphs, I testify to the boundless mercy of a loving and compassionate God.

Nevertheless, I refused to place my trust solely in the doctors' diagnosis of me not being able to give birth again, choosing instead to rely on my unwavering faith. I held steadfast to the belief that the son and daughter I had fervently prayed for would be granted to me. I had the son, and now all I desired was for God to gift me my daughter. So, it was time to stand on the scripture in Matthew 7:7, Ask and it will be given to you; seek and you will find; knock and the door will be opened to you.

When I arrived home, I cradled my son in my arms once more. His presence was an indication of God's faithfulness and the power of prayer. I reminded myself each morning that miraculously, against all odds, I emerged from the dismal situation, surrounded by the prayers of loved ones. I clung to that faith like a lifeline.

But the miraculous story didn't end there. In the months that followed, God continued to work miracles in our lives. Despite what was pronounced over me, I regained strength in my body and did have quality of life.

A little over a year after my son's birth, on June 17, 1983, my husband and I welcomed a beautiful baby girl into the world—a living reminder of God's grace and mercy. The diagnosis the doctor gave me was not my destiny.

What joy my new baby girl brought into our family. My husband and I were blessed with a healthy, handsome boy and now an adorable, healthy baby girl. Can you believe she had a kiss mark on her left cheek? Yes, her birthmark looked like the print of a kiss, and we nicknamed her 'Kisso." What a delight it was for me to raise my son and daughter.

With each passing day, our family grew stronger, guided by the unwavering love of our Heavenly Father. And though the road was not always easy, we trusted in God's plan, knowing that He was always by our side. Our family grew. We had another son, and my children grew up remarkably close to each other. My two sons were incredibly supportive of their sister. If she needed her brothers at any given time or place, they would drop everything to be by her side. And it was reciprocated on her end as well.

Gammy Have You Heard

On Tuesday, June 1, 2021, I joined a prayer call with my pastor and church family at 7:00 PM. About fifteen minutes later, my granddaughter called, her voice tinged with concern as she asked,

"Gammy, have you heard from my mom?" I reassured her that I hadn't heard anything from her mother despite numerous attempts to reach out through calls and texts. "It's unusual for her not to respond," my granddaughter remarked, her worry evident in her tone.

Desperate for any clue to her whereabouts. I quickly instructed my granddaughter to contact my daughter's closest cousin. She had not heard from her either, but my granddaughter could track her mother's location through her cell phone. Moments later, my granddaughter's frantic voice pierced through the telephone, her cries echoing with distress as she relayed the devastating news—her mother had been in an accident. As she arrived at the scene, the sight that greeted her was harrowing—her mother's truck, mangled and wrecked, already being towed away. Amid the chaos, the police offered no solace, leaving us grasping for answers in a sea of uncertainty. With a heavy heart, I urged her to come and pick me up so we could find out what happened together, each passing second fraught with escalating worry.

With trembling hands, I beckoned her to my side, resolved to face this ordeal together upon our arrival at the hospital. A sinking feeling settled in the pit of my stomach as we were met with disbelief—there was no one by her name admitted. I dialed another hospital frantically, only to receive the same disheartening response. The weight of uncertainty bore down upon me, a torrent of stress and fear threatening to overwhelm me. In desperation, I reached out to one of my trusted prayer warriors, their unwavering faith serving as a beacon of hope in our darkest hour. With bated breath, we waited, clinging to the belief that divine intervention would guide us through this frustrating ordeal.

In the fluorescent-lit confines of the hospital waiting room, we sat with our hearts heavy with the unknown as we awaited news of my daughter's fate. The minutes stretched on agonizingly, each one filled with a sense of apprehension and dread. Not knowing where she was or what had happened to her only added to our anxiety, leaving us feeling helpless and powerless in the face of the unknown.

When the news finally came that she had been admitted to the hospital, albeit under a different name, a wave of relief washed over us. She was listed as Jane Doe. That was not understandable, but it was as though a heavy weight had been lifted from our shoulders, and for a brief moment, hope flickered in the darkness. But that hope was short-lived, extinguished by the arrival of a deputy bearing the devastating news that my daughter had been involved in a car crash and had not survived.

The room was filled with the sound of my granddaughter's anguished cries, her grief echoing off the sterile walls. It was a heartbreaking sight, seeing her so utterly devastated by the loss of her mother. As I held her trembling form in my arms, I couldn't help but feel a sense of helplessness wash over me. This wasn't the first time I had comforted someone during tragedy, but it was the first time it had been my own flesh and blood, and the pain felt different somehow.

My daughter had been six months pregnant at the time of the accident, adding another layer of tragedy to an already devastating situation. The shock of her sudden passing reverberated through our family, leaving us reeling in disbelief. As we wrestled with our own grief, we were also forced to confront the pain of my granddaughter, who had lost not only her mother but also the sibling she had been eagerly anticipating.

In the days and weeks that followed, we struggled to come to terms with the enormity of our loss, taking each day as it came and leaning on one another for support. It was a difficult journey, marked by moments of profound sadness and overwhelming grief. But through it all, we clung to the memories of my daughter, finding solace in the love and laughter she had brought into our lives.

As a missionary in the church, I had spent years offering comfort and support to others in their darkest hours, but now it was my turn to lean on the strength and compassion of those around me. Together, we navigated the storm of grief, finding moments of light and hope amidst the darkness. And though the pain of my daughter's loss will always linger, so too will the love and memories she left behind, a beacon of light guiding us through the darkest of times.

Tears blur my vision as I sit here penning this chapter for you, trying to put my thoughts into words. It's still hard to believe she's gone. That dreadful day when my daughter left work at 4:00 p.m., heading to my house, is imprinted into my memory. It was a day like any other until tragedy struck. At 4:20 p.m., she was involved in a head-on collision, and by 6:20 p.m., she had passed away in the hospital.

Later that night, around 10:20 p.m., my family and friends gathered at the hospital, seeking solace in each other's presence. The waiting room was filled with a sense of heaviness as we tried to come to terms with what had happened. Eventually, a nurse led us down a long hallway to see my daughter's lifeless body, a sight that will haunt me forever.

As we walked, I held my granddaughter's hand tightly, trying to find strength in her presence. The hallway seemed endless, illuminated by harsh fluorescent lights that cast eerie shadows on the walls. It felt like a journey into the unknown, each step bringing us closer to the reality of our loss.

In that moment, surrounded by loved ones, I felt a sense of numbness wash over me. It was as if time had stood still, and all I could do was cling to the hope that, somehow, this was all just a bad dream. But as we entered the room where my daughter lay, her stillness spoke volumes, and the truth of her passing hit me like a ton of bricks.

Despite the overwhelming grief that threatened to consume me, I knew I had to be strong for my family. It was a role I never expected to take on, but one I embraced with all my heart. In the days and weeks that followed, we leaned on each other for support, finding comfort in shared memories and knowing we were not alone in our pain.

Nights were spent in restless turmoil, the silence broken only by the sound of my own sobbing and each morning brought with it a harsh reminder of our loss, a stark contrast to the brightness of the world outside. But even in our darkest moments, there were glimpses of light – moments of laughter shared with family and friends, memories that brought a smile to our faces even through tears.

As the days turned into weeks and months, the pain of our loss began to soften, replaced by a bittersweet sense of remembrance. We carried our daughter's memory wherever we went, finding relief in the knowledge that she would always be a part of us. And though the ache of her absence may never fully heal, we take comfort in the love and support of those around us, knowing that we are not alone in our grief.

Oh, the Pain

The grief I experienced was overwhelming, hitting me in diverse ways at different times. Sometimes, I felt numb, like it wasn't real, while other times, the pain was so intense it was hard to bear. Through it all, I clung to my faith, finding comfort in the belief that my suffering had a purpose. My support pillars were my family, church community, pastor, and church leaders, offering their love and prayers unconditionally. Their presence gave me the courage to face each day, knowing I was not alone in my struggles.

I began to have more questions than answers. Therefore, I called the staff at the hospital and needed a meeting to get answers about what my daughter's last words were. They spoke to me for two hours, helping me access my emotions in the healing process.

It became so difficult with the memories of my daughter around my house. Although she had her own home, she visited frequently. I accompanied her every month to her doctor's appointments to watch my granddaughter grow and look at the ultrasounds. My granddaughter was expected to come in September of 2021.

We had a gender reveal party, and my nineteen-year-old granddaughter helped her mom put the baby room together. We had a baby shower, and my daughter received so many gifts. Saddened, we had to return some of the gifts, but we were blessed to give some of the presents to mothers who needed them. It was indeed an emotional roller coaster.

As time went on, the pain of losing my daughter seemed to seep into every corner of my life. Everywhere I looked, I was reminded of her – in the empty chair at the dinner table, in the silence of her room, in the sound of her favorite song playing on the radio. It was as if her absence had left a gaping hole in the fabric of our family, a void that could never be filled.

But amidst the darkness were moments of light—small, fleeting glimpses of hope that reminded me that life still had meaning. It was in my grandchildren's laughter, the warmth of a friend's hug, and the quiet moments of reflection and prayer. These moments kept me going and gave me the strength to face each new day with courage and grace.

And though the pain of losing my daughter will never entirely go away, I take comfort in knowing that she is at peace, that she is watching over us from above. Her memory lives on in the hearts of those who loved her, a beacon of light in the darkness, a reminder that love is eternal and that we are never truly alone.

The weight of sorrow presses upon me like a heavy burden, prompting a temporary retreat from the familiar confines of home to seek solace with family in Atlanta, Georgia, for eleven days. Looking back, subtle signs of impending tragedy emerged, though they went unnoticed until that fateful day. It was May 31, 2021, the day before my daughter's passing, Memorial Day. As my husband and I tended to the barbecue grill in the backyard, she made an unexpected visit. Sharing her plans to visit her cousin's house, she made a point to stop by each of her uncles' homes before heading there, a gesture that only later revealed its true significance. The following day, she was gone.

In the wake of my daughter's passing, I found solace in the unwavering guidance of my Lord and Savior. Through prayer, meditation on His word, and sharing my journey with others, I unearthed a wellspring of strength and compassion that defied human understanding. God's promises, especially to those navigating the penetrable waves of grief, became a steadfast beacon of hope, illuminating the darkest corners of my heart.

Among the ups and downs of sorrow, I sought refuge in the

company of kindred spirits—fellow women and mothers who bore the weight of similar burdens. Over shared meals and heartfelt conversations, we found solace and understanding in one another's stories. As a Christian woman leader within my church community, I took it upon myself to organize seminars and panel discussions on coping with grief and nurturing an environment where individuals could find healing and resilience.

Transformative Power of the Faith Journey

Reflecting on my daughter's enduring legacy, I am flooded with gratitude for the thirty-seven years she graced us with her love and laughter. She had an innate organizational talent, effortlessly coordinating every birthday and holiday celebration for our family and extended kin. Her meticulous planning and systematic approach were invaluable within our family and Mesias Temple Church's confines, where her contributions were indispensable.

One particularly cherished memory is her tireless efforts in organizing the backpacks for the Back-to-School drives and establishing essential supplies for both our church and the neighboring community. Additionally, as a tribute to my mother, her leadership in the annual Breast Cancer Awareness walk showcased her compassionate spirit and unwavering commitment to serving others. During Resurrection weekend, she brought joy to families through Easter egg hunt festivities, fostering a sense of community and togetherness.

The void left by her absence remains palpable, a testament to the profound impact she had on the lives of countless individuals, extending far beyond our immediate family. Each day, I honor her memory by embracing the legacy of love and service she embodied. Though grief lingers, I find solace in the belief that she now resides in the gentle embrace of our Heavenly Father, her spirit forever woven into the tapestry of our lives.

I offer words of encouragement and guidance for those embarking on their own journey of grief and healing. Embrace faith as a source of strength and solace, entrusting your burdens to Christ and finding support in the love of family and friends. Open communication within your community is essential, fostering empathy and understanding in the face of loss and sorrow.

Above all, I implore you to embrace the transformative power of faith, finding redemption and renewal in the promise of eternal life. Through Him, we discover the courage to traverse the darkest valleys and emerge into the radiant light of healing and hope. In the intricate walk of life, moments of sorrow are fused alongside threads of faith, binding us together in love and resilience. As we navigate the complexities of grief, may we find comfort in knowing that we are never alone, for God's love surrounds us, guiding us through the darkest nights.

As I journey through the depths of grief, I am reminded of the importance of cherishing the memories we hold dear. In the quiet moments of reflection, I find solace in the happiness shared, the cries, and the passion that continues to bind us together, even in death. Though the pain may never fully fade, the memories we hold dear serve as a lighthouse, guiding us through the darkest of nights.

Amid tragedy, it can be easy to lose sight of the blessings surrounding us. Yet, even in the depths of sorrow, there is beauty to be found—in the kindness of strangers, the embrace of loved ones, and the unwavering grace of our Heavenly Father. As we journey through the valley of grief, may we hold fast to the hope that lies beyond the horizon, knowing that even in our darkest hour, we are never alone.

As I reflect on the journey ahead, I am reminded of Psalm 30:5, "Weeping may endure for a night, but joy comes in the morning." Though the road may be long and the pain may run deep, I take comfort in knowing that joy awaits us on the other side of sorrow. In the meantime, I hold fast to the promise of God's love, knowing He will carry us through the darkest of nights and lead us into the light of a new day.

Looking back on those difficult days, I am reminded of God's faithfulness and the power of prayer. He heard our cries and answered them in ways we never could have imagined. And through it all, His love sustained us, bringing light into the darkest times. So, to all facing trials and tribulations, I offer this message of hope—trust in God's plan, for He is faithful to see us through even the darkest days. With Him by our side, we can overcome any obstacle and emerge stronger than before.

Ruby Bostic and her husband Anthony Bostic Sr. are proud parents of three grown children: Anthony Jr. (married to Ashley), LaCrystal (deceased), Jerrell, and Carlis. They also cherish four grandchildren: Megan, D'mere, Amon, and Avery, with another grandchild expected in October 2024. Ruby's journey with faith began at Messias Temple Church in 1972, where she was baptized in 1973 and received the Holy Ghost in 1974.

Recognizing her calling to ministry, Ruby has served her church since 2005, teaching Sunday School and leading as Missionary President since 2006. Her responsibilities include visiting convalescent homes and hospitals and comforting the bereaved and sick. Ruby's commitment to personal growth led her to Wayne County Community College from 2010 to 2012, where she earned certifications including Aenon Ministerial Introduction (2004), Dale Carnegie (2005), and Aenon Ministerial License from PAW (2010). Through her service and unwavering faith, Ruby continues to inspire and impact her community positively.

“Don't underestimate yourself. You are capable of more than you can ever imagine.”

-Les Brown

A MOTHER'S LOSS

On that unforgettable day, June 22, 2023, our world was shattered by the sudden loss of our beloved firstborn and sole son, Kaelin Howard Cason, at the tender age of twenty-eight. He left behind a legacy as a devoted father to three young ones and a pillar of strength for his two adoring younger sisters, Ashanti, aged twenty-three, and Keauna, just twenty.

I recall vividly the scene in our home office that day, enveloped in the routine task of scanning my student identification verification form for Walden University—an obligation I had intended to fulfill the week prior but had been delayed due to a much-needed family vacation in Turks & Caicos. Then, my husband, Ernest (affectionately known as Lovey), glanced out the window and gently informed me that my younger brother Derrick had just arrived.

I asked Lovey if he was expecting him, and he said no. When my brother parked his truck and got out, I noticed my sister-in-law, Alicia, was with him. Lovey also noticed and said, "Oh, they (my brother and sister-in-law) must have found a house in our neighborhood. In my head, I remember thinking: I don't have time to chit-chat, so this one is on Lovey.

As I continued to get my papers together to scan to the office, Lovey opened the door, and they came inside. Intending to say hello and let them know I was on a tight schedule, I went out into the hallway to speak to them, and I immediately noticed they did not look like the happy and fun-loving couple they were. I thought, "Uh-oh, they look intense. Are they breaking up?" But that thought was directly followed by, "If they were breaking up, they both wouldn't come," so I figured it had something to do with them looking for a house. After greeting and hugging each other, Lovey said, "Y'all must have found a house." Derrick said, "No." So I looked at Alicia and asked excitedly, "Are you pregnant?" She looked shocked and said, "God no" (they are a blended family with three children combined).

Derrick looked at my husband and me and said, "We have some bad news about Kaelin," I responded, "What happened?" Derrick looked at me and then looked at Lovey and said, "he got shot in the back." I remember sucking my breath in and asking Derrick, "Where is he?" because I was ready to go to him.

I remember Derrick looking between my husband and me, saying one of three things. He either said, "He didn't make it; he passed away, or he died." I immediately said, "Oh, I know you are lying!" and went into the office and hyperventilated. I was like, "No, they have this mixed up… they have the wrong person… this is mistaken identity." I heard my husband ask him how he knew it was Kaelin, and Derrick said his girlfriend identified him. I was still in the office and kept saying, "No, this is wrong; they have the wrong person." The next thing I heard was my husband yell, "F***!"

I came out of the office, and Lovey wanted to hug me, but I didn't want to touch him or anyone else. I remember thinking, "If I cry and fall apart, that makes this real, and it isn't real because how could he be dead?" We decided we were going to go to the morgue and see for ourselves if they had the right person or not, but we were not able to go because once the county claimed and identified the body, we were not allowed to see it. At that point, arrangements would have to be made with the funeral home.

The Notifications

Kaelin was not just our child but also a big brother. Our oldest daughter, Ashanti, was home when my brother came to deliver the news. I didn't know he went upstairs and asked her to keep Isaiah (our grandson) upstairs because he needed to talk to us about Kaelin.

Our youngest daughter happened to come home while Derrick and Alicia were still there, and she sensed that something was going on because we were all just standing around looking very tense and serious. We figured we needed to tell them that their brother was dead, so my husband walked upstairs to talk to them. Ashanti came downstairs before he went upstairs, but Keauna didn't come down. When Lovey told her he needed to speak to her about Kaelin, she started crying, saying she didn't want to know. I could hear her crying while he was talking to her, and I remember Ashanti looking at me and asking if I was okay. I can't remember what I said, but I was in shock and total disbelief.

Lovey felt it was important for him to go and tell the mother of Kaelin's two oldest children what happened. I stayed home because his youngest child, our only grandson, lives with us. Our daughters decided to go with him for support if it was too hard for him. I remember sitting on the couch trying to make sense of it and saying there must have been a mistake because none of this made any sense.

Around 9:15 pm, a knock at our door heralded the arrival of two police chaplains, and my composure crumbled instantly. I stood at the threshold, my emotions raw, insisting that they weren't welcome and that I hadn't summoned them. Their uncertain expressions mirrored my distress. As my brother approached, I uttered in anguish, "Your presence makes this all too real."

One of the chaplains, sensing my need, enveloped me in a comforting embrace, and we swayed together in solace. The time they were blurred in our embrace until we retreated to the living room, where I surrendered to tears. They shared details of their support services for grieving families, leaving behind their cards with a gentle offer to reach out if I required any assistance.

After the chaplains left, my husband and daughters came home, and we turned the TV on to see if the local news reported the story. We were concerned that Kaelin's name would be mentioned, and no one in our families knew except my brother and sister-in-law.

Sitting in Disbelief

The news report was aired, omitting his name while detailing the grim circumstances of his death. It seemed he was fatally shot from behind near a park, and there were no witnesses, no suspects. As the limited details unfolded, I clung to a desperate hope that a call would come, dispelling this nightmare with news of a colossal misunderstanding that our son was indeed alive. The emotions swirling within me at that moment and persisting to this day defy articulation. That night marked the onset of a relentless bout of insomnia, my mind unable to find solace in sleep.

Throughout the remaining hours, I sat in a suspended state of disbelief and anguish, grappling with the void left by unanswered questions. The weight of uncertainty pressed heavily upon me, a relentless ache echoing the heart-wrenching reality of his absence. Insomnia became my unwelcome companion, tethering me to the night with restless thoughts and yearnings for a resolution that seemed perpetually out of reach.

As I sat and replayed his life, I found every mistake I ever made and let the guilt fester, admonishing myself for not being a better mother. Did I say I loved him enough? Did he know I loved him? Was it because he felt it or because I said it? Did I hug him enough? Did he know he was important to me? Did I have to fuss so much? Were we too strict? These questions plagued me for many nights, and if I am being honest, some still do.

Articulate Kaelin

When Kaelin was little, he cried about everything. When I say everything… I mean everything. Now, I can laugh at how he cried a lot, but when he was younger, it drove me crazy. I would ask him why he was crying, and he would always say, "For no reason," to which I would say, "Okay then, stop crying."

When he would get in his mood, his grandmother Vivian would say he was being cantankerous, and it was almost like he knew exactly what that word meant because the look on his face was not contrite but more on the "I don't give a damn" side. He was very strong-willed and stubborn, to say the least. But he was also a very fun-loving little kid with the silliest laugh. He had the kind of laugh that made you smile because his eyes would light up, and you could almost feel the joy he was experiencing.

I remember when he was about two years old, my husband yelled, "Sh*t!" and Kaelin started hopping up and down the hallway repeating the word over and over again. Whenever he would hear his father curse, he made sure to repeat it "ad nauseum" or to a sickening degree.

Kaelin was very articulate. He would hold conversations with people, and they would be amazed at some of the things he would say. One of my uncles once told me, "You guys talk to him a lot, huh?" I laughed because that was his way of telling me that Kaelin talked a lot, which he did. Sometimes I had to say, "Son, take a breather." He would say "Okay" and stop talking for about 30 seconds to pick right back up where he left off. He used to call my uncle, the pastor of our church, Jesus. I remember the first time he said it. We were at my grandmother's house, and my uncle (who was also a mail carrier) walked in the door. After everyone said their greeting, Kaelin turned the corner and said, "Hi Jesus." We all stopped and looked at Kaelin, who was looking at my uncle. Since there was no response, Kaelin said, "Hi Jesus" again, and this time, we knew he was referring to my uncle. My Uncle said, "No, I'm not Jesus. I'm Uncle Darrell." Kaelin looked so confused, and he turned and looked at me. I had to explain that Uncle Darrell wasn't Jesus; he taught us about Jesus. That satisfied Kaelin for the moment, but the next time he saw Uncle Darrell, he called him Jesus again. I thought it was so cute.

I remember his first day of preschool. I was so nervous. I didn't know how he would like it and if he would cry or be to himself. Well, it turns out I had nothing to worry about because before I could even leave the classroom, he was having a ball with the other kids standing on the table dancing. I should have known then we were going to have a few challenges.

Kaelin liked school, just not for all the right reasons. He loved going to school to see his friends but not to learn. The challenging part was he knew the work. Kaelin was brilliant, and because the work came easy, he wasn't being challenged, which contributed to his not paying attention. After talking with his teachers and administrators at the school, we allowed them to put him up (skip a grade). That would come back to haunt us because though he excelled in academics, socially, he was still very immature.

Since first grade, he developed a pattern of playing the first semester of school and buckling down the second semester. He was never in danger of failing because he knew the subject matter. But it frustrated us and the teachers to no end. My husband and I ensured we closely interacted with all his teachers. They had our cell phone numbers and email addresses so they could reach out at any time, and thankfully, they did.

One of the main complaints we received was that Kaelin wasn't doing his homework. We were like, that's not true because we sat here and ensured it was done. It turns out he was doing his homework, but he wasn't turning it in. He would either crumple it up and stick it in the bottom of his backpack or stuff it in his desk at school. We never understood why he would do that, especially after spending so much time doing it. Well, that became a pattern with him. So, for the next 12 years, we were on a rollercoaster ride with Kaelin and school. As I stated earlier, his teachers were frustrated and very baffled because he knew the work but wouldn't do it.

I remember feeling bad for our son because all of his cousins had brothers, and he was the only boy with sisters. He thoroughly enjoyed visiting my brother's house to hang out with his cousins. Those were some of the happiest I had seen him because he was with boys his age (he is five years older than Ashanti and eight years older than Keauna). My oldest brother was into music and created the gospel rap group The Messengers with Kaelin, his youngest son, and another cousin. The Messengers performed at local events in Sacramento and the Bay Area. They were somewhat like local celebrities because people had heard about them everywhere they went. There was no turning back after that. Music became his first love.

Once he graduated from high school, Kaelin wanted to be out and about. He loved being in Sacramento, living his life, and away from home where the rules still applied though he was an adult. He enrolled in college but decided it wasn't what he wanted to do, so he looked for jobs where he could cook (his second love). He would put dishes together that didn't seem like they would complement each other, but they did. Whenever he came over, I would tell him to make me some salsa without the jalapenos because his was my favorite. He was super excited when he became an entrepreneur and started a cooking venture business with some other young men. He was the chef, and he was proud. They would do pop-ups and post the food on social media. Making sure we supported him; my husband would go to their spot and pick up a few things. He was immensely proud of that accomplishment, and so were we.

As much as he loved cooking and music, nothing compared to his joy of fatherhood. When he was growing up, I always stressed that I wanted him to wait to have sex AND children until he was married. Of course, he would look at me as if to say, "Silly lady, that's not going to happen."

I remember when he called to tell us that we would be grandparents. He asked if his dad was home. I told him to call the cell phone because his dad was at volleyball practice. He said he wanted to talk to both of us, and I said, "You better not be calling to tell me someone is pregnant." The line was quiet. I yelled, "Kaelin! Someone is pregnant?" He said, "Yes." I couldn't believe it. So, of course, I went into momma lecture mode about using protection and what the future holds. He just laughed me off and told me to chill. So, our first grandchild was born, and 17 months later, our second grandchild was born. I remember telling him to slow down; he needed to wait until marriage. He informed me he wanted a son, so he would keep trying. He got his wish almost three years later; he had a son.

Kaelin was diagnosed with schizoaffective bipolar disorder in 2022. During his adolescence, he began to struggle with anger management, and he went to therapy bi-weekly to learn different coping skills. As an adult, he self-medicated, which, I believe, exacerbated his emotions. As a parent, it is tough to see your child struggle and not be able to help.

My world stopped when Kaelin died. Even writing this chapter, I am still in a space of denial. I still can't believe that our oldest and only son is no longer here.

Vacillating Through the Stages of Grief

Grief is peculiar because it will have you trying to change the outcome of an unchangeable situation. I remember thinking it was a mistake, praying that it was not real, and trying to sit in a space of accepting life as it now is. I still can't fully process what we went through. Most of the time, I feel our experience was a movie or show I watched on television, and I am waiting for the finale to tie everything together and make it right. Unfortunately, that episode will never come.

I vacillate between being depressed, angry, and in denial. I see his face in everything I do, and sometimes, the feelings are so overwhelming I want to scream and break things. When I drive down the street and see a skinny, light-skinned, curly-haired young man, I do a double take to see if that is my son.

Grief is not linear; it's all over the place, and that is the only way I can describe my emotions. I am, however, thankful for the support I have around me. I am not sure if it is fortunate or unfortunate that I have a community of other sisters who have also lost their sons. Being in their company and seeing that they didn't crumple and stop living has helped me push on. There has been encouragement to join or start a support group, but I am not there yet. As silly as it may sound, seeing someone for grief counseling makes this official: the sale is final, and there are no returns. Like I said, silly, right?

The Asterisk

There is an asterisk for everything that happened after 3:30 pm on June 22, 2023, because it signifies the changes in our family dynamic. We will never be whole because there will never be five of us again. The new normal feels incomplete because we are missing a piece of the puzzle that will never return. My new normal is filled with anxiety because whenever our daughters are out and about, I worry more than I used to, and I wait for them to come home.

I stress out when I meet people because I am not well-versed in how to say, "My son died." Grant it; I don't just come out and volunteer that information, but eventually, the question comes up about our children. Being polite, people ask the standard "how many kids, ages, still at home or not, etc." questions.

Though I am plagued with guilt about things I should have done differently, I find solace in the last conversation I had with Kaelin. We spoke of love. I told him I loved him and was looking forward to seeing him later (he was supposed to come home that evening). He said he loved me too and he would see me later. We said goodbye, and that was it. I'm so glad we had that time; it is another thing for which I am grateful to The Lord. I am also thankful that I have two voice messages saved on my phone from him. One was from him calling to tell me happy birthday, and another was to say hi because he was thinking about me. I play those often and smile because I hear him smiling into the phone. I am also grateful for all of the pictures we have taken together. When he was younger, he didn't like taking pictures, but as he got older, he and I would take silly pictures together.

There is a community of people that we know who have lost their children before they were able to become grandparents, so I understand that we are very blessed that we have three grandchildren to love. We aren't just left with a memory, but something tangible that we have left of Kaelin. We get to kiss, hug, and squeeze them while marveling at how we see our son in each of them.

The oldest granddaughter has her father's serious and focused demeanor. When Kaelin was focused, it was laser, and I remember at times having to snap my fingers or clap my hands to get his attention. Our middle granddaughter has his laughter. She can light up a room with the same smile and laugh as her father, and our youngest and only grandson looks exactly like his father.

They are all highly creative and have an imagination, just like their father. I am honored that The Lord saw fit to bless us with them. We have fun with them, whether playing, watching movies, or running around the house.

I have been waiting to wake up from this nightmare since 6:00 pm on June 22, 2023. Most days, I feel like I am having an out-of-body experience when I think of my brother delivering the news that our son is gone. I think about all the things he will miss seeing his children grow up and all the things we will miss.

The story wasn't supposed to end this way because it feels unfinished. I understand and recognize that grief is a process. Every day, I wake up in denial. I move to anger and then settle in at depression. This is my life cycle for now. The last step of acceptance has alluded me, and I am unsure if or when it will catch me.

Ronna "Snooks" Cason, MSW, is an inspirational Marriage Mentor that co-hosts the Most Impactful Marriage Podcast in the World, "Married Into Crazy®," with her groom of 27+ years. As a keynote speaker, marriage advocate, Couple 2 Couple Coach, author, dedicated wife, and mother, Ronna uses her Extreme Execution training along with Level 1&2 Gottman Method Couples Therapy Certifications to serve marriages around the world. She and her dedicated husband help couples overcome adversity in their marriages and build bridges to lasting and loving relationships through their C.R.A.Z.Y. Couple method. CRAZY = Compassionate, Real, Accountable, Zealous, Yielding. They have one son (Forever 28), two daughters, and 3 grandchildren.

Visit www.MarriedIntoCrazy.com to learn more about how she supports marriage worldwide.

"Grief is like the ocean; it comes in waves, ebbing and flowing. Sometimes the water is calm, and sometimes it is overwhelming. All we can do is learn to swim."

-Vicki Harrison

TREASURY and A MOTHER'S LOVE

A woman giving birth to a child has pain because her time has come, but when her baby is born, she forgets the anguish because of her joy that a child is born into the world. John 16:21 NIV

A Mother's Love

When your child is born, a world of emotions explodes within you, each more powerful than the last. You hold your newborn for the first time, feeling an overwhelming rush of love that leaves you breathless. Every tiny feature—each delicate finger, every soft sigh—fills you with awe and wonder. You marvel at this little miracle you've brought into the world. As you softly murmur your first hello, your mind begins to dance with visions of the future. You imagine the first smile that will light up your world, the infectious laughter that will echo through your home, and the sweet sound of your child calling you "Mom" or "Dad."

You envision their tentative first steps, the look of pure joy and curiosity as they begin to explore their surroundings. You see their first day of school, the blend of excitement and nervousness as they grip your hand tightly, and the swell of pride you'll feel as they bravely step into their classroom. The years rush by in your mind, leading to their prom night, where they stand before you, radiant and on the cusp of adulthood. You picture their wedding day, tears of happiness blurring your vision as you watch them begin a new chapter of love and life. And in the golden years, you see yourself on a peaceful porch, the air filled with the laughter of grandchildren playing—a living demonstration of the love and legacy you've nurtured.

As you cradle this precious new life, you can't help but dream about what lies ahead. Will your bundle of joy become a doctor, saving lives with their skill and compassion? Or perhaps a lawyer advocating for justice with unyielding conviction? You thank God for the immense privilege of parenthood, for the honor of guiding this new soul, and you silently pray for the wisdom and strength to fulfill this sacred duty. Yet, amid all these joyous thoughts, there is one possibility you refuse to contemplate. The idea that all this profound love could one day turn into unimaginable pain if your child were to leave this world before you is simply too unbearable. It is a reality that defies the natural order, a heart-wrenching notion that you cannot and will not fathom. It is a chapter you hope never to write in your life story, a shadow you pray never darkens your door. The mere whisper of such a loss is a shadow you desperately wish to keep away, a pain you fervently hope never to endure.

On November 9, 1992, at precisely 4:26 pm, I welcomed my second child into the world. She was a breathtakingly beautiful 6-pound, 9-ounce baby girl, her brown skin glowing with the promise of life. Her eyes were the deepest brown I had ever seen, vast pools that seemed to hold the world's mysteries. What left me utterly baffled was her jet-black hair—thick and luscious on the top of her head yet conspicuously absent at the back. It was as if she had come into this world with a little secret, a unique quirk that made her even more special.

My two-year-old son was captivated by his new sister. He examined her tiny fingers with innocent curiosity, marveling at their perfection. He kissed her hand with the tenderness only a sibling could possess. His face lit up with excitement as he tried to hold her, his little hands gently attempting to smooth down the stubborn strand of hair that refused to lay flat at her hairline. She was his first little sister, his newfound companion in the adventure of life, and my first little princess. To us, she was perfect. I named her Treasury, for she was indeed a treasure beyond measure.

As the years passed, it became clear that Treasury's life would not be easy. In her late teens, she was diagnosed with a mental disability that made everyday life a constant struggle. Her mind, a battlefield of conflicting thoughts and emotions, played relentless tricks on her. Yet, no matter how fierce the internal storm, it could never dim the light of her intelligence or vibrant personality. Treasury was a whirlwind of energy, her presence so loud and funny that you couldn't help but laugh and shake your head at her antics. Those head shakes were often followed by a chuckling and the statements: "Shut up, Treasury" or a playful "Go home Treasury."

Treasury fought valiantly every day to live a better life than the one her illness tried to impose on her. She mastered many hobbies but found true joy in braiding hair. She dedicated countless hours to perfecting her craft, transforming it into an art form. Her nimble fingers wove intricate patterns, each braid a proof of her determination and skill. Treasury's most incredible pride, however, was being a mother. She gave birth to three children—two boys and one girl. Motherhood was her crowning achievement, the role she cherished above all others. She poured her heart and soul into being the best mother she could be, working tirelessly to provide for and nurture her children.

Tragically, on the evening of October 31, 2022, Treasury's life was cut short in the most horrific manner. She was shot and killed in her home while preparing dinner for herself and her youngest child. The violence of that night shattered our world. My grandson, though physically unharmed, was left with a trauma that words cannot fully capture. The loss of Treasury was a blow that struck deep into the core of our family, a wound that will forever ache.

Though fraught with challenges, Treasury's life was a beacon of resilience and love. Her memory lives on in the hearts of those who knew her, a testament to a spirit that refused to be dimmed by adversity. She was, and always will be, our treasure.

A Mother's Pain

My youngest daughter called me around 10 pm that night and told me Treasury had been killed. At first, I couldn't believe her. I repeatedly asked her, "Where is Treasury?" as if her answer might change somehow. I could hear her voice speaking, but my mind simply refused to process the devastating news. It felt like an alternate reality where such a tragedy couldn't be true. The world I knew and understood seemed to crumble around me, leaving me in a void of disbelief and despair.

When I arrived at Treasury's apartment, it was chaotic and sorrowful. I didn't see the buildings or the people milling around in shock; my vision tunneled in on the emergency vehicles' flashing blue and red lights. Those lights painted the world in harsh, alternating colors, making everything feel surreal. My heart began to hurt so intensely; it felt as though it was being squeezed by an invisible vice. I couldn't hear anything beyond the rushing blood in my ears, and breathing became an impossible task. It was as if every drop of air had been sucked out of my body and replaced with an unbearable, all-consuming pain.

My mind and skin hurt, every organ in my body hurt. It was a pain so profound, so unimaginable, that I hadn't known such a depth of suffering could exist. Treasury was really gone. In an instant, my beautiful, brown-skinned baby girl had been reduced to a memory, a haunting echo of the vibrant life she once had. The thought was inconceivable, a nightmare I desperately wanted to wake from, yet there was no escape from this new, harsh reality.

I had 10,948 days of memories with her, but at that moment, the pain was so overwhelming that it would not even allow me to recall a single one. I desperately tried to summon her image and hear her voice, but I couldn't. My mind was a vast, dark void, empty of the comforting recollections I needed. It seemed to stay that way forever until only one thought broke through the darkness: where is my grandson?

That singular thought gripped me with a terror and urgency that words fail to capture. My mind raced with a thousand fears, each one more horrifying than the last. I honestly can't say what thoughts or emotions took over then because they were beyond articulation. They were raw, unusual feelings that tore into my soul. The fear for my grandson's safety overshadowed everything else, pulling me further into a tornado of anxiety and dread.

Death had already claimed my grandmother, a woman of strength and wisdom who had been the bedrock of our family. It had just recently taken my father, a loss that had left a gaping hole in my heart. And now, on the night it came for one of my babies, I stood there not knowing if it had also come for one of hers. The weight of that uncertainty was crushing. It was as if the world had collapsed inward, and I was standing at the epicenter of unimaginable grief and fear.

I felt utterly alone at that moment, surrounded by people yet isolated in my pain. The world continued moving around me, but I was frozen in time, trapped in a nightmare I couldn't wake. Every second stretched into an eternity as I grappled with the horrific reality that had been thrust upon me. My soul screamed in anguish, a soundless cry that echoed within the confines of my heart. The pain was unrelenting, an inescapable torment that defied comprehension.

As I stood there, a mother shattered, I realized my love for Treasury was a double-edged sword. It had brought me immense joy, but now it was the source of a deep sorrow that felt like it would consume me. The memories, once a source of comfort, were now a reminder of what I had lost. Treasury was gone, and with her, a piece of my heart that could never be replaced.

I thought back to the early days when I first held her, how her tiny hand would grasp my finger so tightly, the warmth of her little body against mine. I remembered her laughter, a sound so pure and full of life that it could brighten the darkest days. These memories, once cherished, now felt like daggers, each slicing through my soul's fragile remnants.

The agony of knowing I would never again see her smile, hear her voice, or feel her embrace was a burden too heavy to bear. I looked around at the flashing lights, the bustling emergency personnel, and the growing crowd of onlookers, and it all seemed so distant, so disconnected from the immediate gut pain I was experiencing.

Amid this commotion, a police officer approached me, his face a mask of professional sympathy. He spoke, but the roar of my own grief drowned out his words. I could see his lips moving and could sense the gravity of what he was saying, but it felt like trying to understand a foreign language. Nothing made sense anymore; the world had tilted on its axis, and I struggled to find my footing in this new, brutal reality.

My thoughts kept circling back to my grandson. Was he safe? Had he seen what happened? The idea of him witnessing such a violent act filled me with a fresh wave of nausea and fear. I needed to find, hold, and assure him that he was not alone despite the horror. But I was as lost as he might have been in that moment, drifting in a sea of sorrow and uncertainty, and the minutes dragged on, each one feeling like an hour, as I stood there, immobilized by grief. People moved around me, talking, crying, shouting, but their sounds were muted as if I were underwater. My whole body ached with the weight of the loss, a physical display of the emotional devastation within.

Eventually, I was led away from the scene, but the pain followed me, a relentless companion that clung to my every step. In the days that followed, I would come to understand that this pain, this unbearable ache, was now a permanent part of me. It was the price of love, the dark side of the immense joy Treasury had brought into my life. And though it threatened to consume me, I knew I had to find a way to keep going—for my family, for my grandson, and the memory of my beautiful, irreplaceable daughter.

Faith

> *The Lord is close to the brokenhearted; he rescues those whose spirits are crushed. - Psalm 34:18 NLT*

Here is the thing about God: you can't lock Him up anywhere. Even if you push Him aside, whether intentionally or unintentionally, He is always there. Soon, my phone stopped ringing, and there were no more visitors to turn away from or anyone who needed convincing to know that I was okay. My world grew quiet, and a thought crept into my mind in that silence: I AM NOT SUPPOSED TO OUTLIVE MY CHILDREN. As those words settled in my consciousness, I felt utterly broken, alone, and completely defeated. It was in that moment of profound despair that God made His presence known.

I didn't hear any physical words, but my heart relaxed just enough to let my lungs fill with a sense of warmth. I suddenly felt as if I had too much air, and as I closed my eyes, I called out to Him. I cried, and I talked to God. He opened that internal door that contained those 10,948 days of memories. I thanked Him, I cried, I cried more, and I talked to God.

Soon, I could think back to the worst moment of my life and recognize how present God was during that time. When my body went into autopilot mode the week after Treasury's death, God WAS the autopilot. He guided me in every decision I made. He placed family and friends exactly where they needed to be to handle everything that I couldn't. He protected my son and grandson, who had no lasting damage from their seizures. He never left me.

Do I believe I lost faith? No. I think the intense emotions and the level of pain I was experiencing while still feeling the need to be strong for everyone was more than I could handle physically and mentally. This forced me to lock it all away and block it out, disabling my ability to cry out. I kept it bottled up and became lost within myself. God knows my heart, and He took over... autopilot.

Grief is different for everyone. It is different according to who you've lost. I couldn't process the death of my daughter the way I did my father and grandmother. Treasury's death unleashed a surge of emotions all at once. It produced grief fueled by as much anger as it did love. It contained guilt because she died alone. I'm her mother—did she call out for me to help her? It contained fear, the fear that every situation my children are involved in will end the same way October 31, 2022, did.

My relationship with God helps me to be a little stronger every day, which has allowed me to take the necessary steps to start handling my grief differently. These are baby steps, but they are steps moving forward and no longer just standing still. For this, I am thankful.

Acceptance

It has been a little over a year and a half since Treasury was taken from us. I would like to say there is less pain now, but that would be a lie. Grief is a pain that will never completely go away. Some days, I can make it through without crying, but as soon as night falls, so do the tears. Other days start and end in tears. I will say the crying spells have shortened a little bit, but as of now, I deal with them day by day.

Yes, I've had memories without tears. That was a tough one to conquer, but it is one I continue to work on the hardest. I must be able to share my memories with her children. They are young and have so few of their own. Her youngest loves hearing stories about his mother going through something similar to what he is experiencing. I tell the story to God first. Yes, I know He already knows it. Telling it to God first helps me process the memory so that I can share it with him.

I sometimes catch myself talking to Treasury. I decided to write the conversations down instead of just talking to the air, so I am now journaling. I call it my "Conversations with Treasury." It contains things I didn't get the chance to say and things she already knows. This is one of the baby steps to dealing with my grief. It is extremely helpful on those days when my emotions are overwhelming. I am making a journal with lots of room for pictures for my grandson so he can start a "Conversation with Mom" journal.

Music has always been a way for me to escape, but now I play certain songs that I didn't listen to before—not because I suddenly liked the song, but because Treasury did. When I play a song that she liked, my grandson always has a story to accompany it. So, I get to hear one of his memories and see the biggest smile while he is telling it.

I am currently working on getting the details of a project out of my head and onto paper so it can be carried out this year. It is a remembrance project for Treasury. I need to do this for myself as well. I am claiming in Jesus' name that as of the day you read this, it will be more than just a vision.

Treasury's death is still fresh for me. It remains hard to talk about, and I know my heart will never be completely healed of the pain. I will no longer ask myself why it still hurts so much because grief has no time frame. I know it will get a little easier every day with God's grace. I will one day be able to say I'm okay truthfully.

To those walking a similar path of grief, know that it's okay not to be alright. Allow yourself the time and space to grieve in your own way. Lean on your faith and the people around you who offer support and love. Please write down your thoughts, talk them out, and find small projects that give you purpose and connection to their memory.

Remember, it's the small steps forward, no matter how tiny, that count. Embrace the memories, cry when needed, and let yourself heal at your own pace. With God's grace, you will find moments of peace and progress.

Rashon Itson is a true country soul. Born in Flint, MI, she was raised in the serene landscapes of Mississippi and Tennessee. Her educational path includes Beecher Community School, Mott College, and Purdue University, where she pursued studies in Culinary Arts and Business Administration.

With her late husband, they have nine children and twenty grandchildren. Her joys include pleasing God Almighty, cherishing family moments, indulging in watching Criminal Minds, and swaying to the tunes of Tim McGraw.

"Hope is being able to see that there is light despite all of the darkness."
-Desmond Tutu

FATHERHOOD IS MORE THAN BIOLOGY

"What's wrong?" I questioned cautiously; my heart skipped a beat at the unfamiliar urgency in my wife's voice. Her frantic footsteps shattered the evening calm, abruptly pulling me from the mundane task of chopping vegetables for dinner. Startled, I wiped my hands on a dish towel and turned to face her, a sense of menacing confusion creeping over me.

"They said Jesse is dead," she responded, her words hitting me like a thunderbolt. "He's been found dead in an apartment."

The knife slipped from my grip, clattering onto the cutting board as my hands froze in disbelief. Jesse—my son, technically, my stepson, but never a distinction I made in my heart. He was only twenty-six, full of life and dreams. The room spun around me as I struggled to comprehend the devastating news. Parents aren't supposed to bury their children. It violates the natural order—a wound that cuts deeper than words could express.

Won Through Food

Memories flooded my mind, transporting me back to the first time I saw Jesse's face —a shy twelve-year-old boy who stole my heart over a meal. I met Jesse one month after I started dating his mother. I still remember that evening vividly. It was a date with my new future children. My wife and I had a long-distance relationship, and they came to visit me. They were staying at a local hotel, so I prepared dinner, eager to make a good impression.

Jesse and his sister, Imani, eyed me cautiously as we ate. I assume they were trying to determine my intentions with their mom. But even before they took their first bites, their faces lit up with delight; I had prepared each of their favorite foods, down to the favorite drink and Jesse's love for Hawaiian rolls. During my phone calls with their mom, I listened attentively to the little things about each of them.

When they bit into that food, I knew I had won them over through their stomachs. I can still recall the delight on their faces as they took their first bites, their skepticism melting away with each flavorful dish. From that day on, he was my son—my Jesse. What a great recollection; for a second, I lost the shock of the news and reminisced.

Jesse loved food, and I loved cooking for him. Our kitchen became a sanctuary filled with laughter and the tantalizing aromas of our shared meals. He was my taste tester, my biggest food critic, and my most enthusiastic supporter. Being his Pops was a privilege I cherished every day. Now, standing in the kitchen with the earpiece pressed in my ear as the family began to call, I felt a void opening up inside me, threatening to swallow everything. My late mother's words took on new meaning. Maybe I was in Jesse's life to be a father, to guide him through the challenges of his illness, to support him as he chased his dreams.

My mother's words echoed in my mind. 'You're in his life for a purpose,' she had said, her eyes filled with a knowing seriousness. Back then, we didn't fully understand that purpose, but as the years passed and we faced Jesse's diagnosis, it became clear that my role in his life was deeper than I had ever imagined. Just nine months after my marriage to his mother, he was met with a disruption to his teenage life. None of that mattered; I dealt with the highs and the lows, and he had my heart. My mother knew that.

Like I said, Jesse wasn't just a stepson—he was my heart, living and breathing outside of my own body. Late nights at the ER, countless hospitalizations, and conversations that changed from moment to moment were a part of my world, as were the typical teenage talks about girls, football, and basketball practice and games. His mom's responsibility was my responsibility; we shared the joy of parenthood.

The concept of your heart walking outside your body is profound. It's the feeling of loving someone so deeply that their joy becomes your joy, their pain your pain. Even though Jesse had a great relationship with his dad, he embodied this connection with me. He allowed me to be significant to him. From the moment he came into my life, he became an extension of my being, intertwined with my hopes, dreams, and fears. He allowed me to be a meaningful voice in his life, more than an agreement on a wedding day.

Cooking Through Grief

In the days that followed my son's passing, the kitchen became my sanctuary; in all honesty, it still is and always has been. But now, it is a place where I can concentrate my grief into something tangible. Cooking became my therapy, my way of honoring Jesse's memory with every meal prepared.

I cooked incessantly, preparing his favorite dishes to keep a piece of him alive. Each slice of the knife, each sizzle of the pan, carried with it a bittersweet reminder of our shared love for food and the joy we found in simple moments together. Once alive with Jesse's laughter and playful banter, the kitchen now echoed with emptiness. His absence was profound, a silent void that could have threatened to consume me. But through the act of cooking, I found a sense of purpose—a way to express my love for my son and preserve his memory in the most intimate way possible.

As I diced onions and stirred pots, memories of our culinary adventures flooded my mind. Jesse's infectious interest in trying new flavors and his discerning palate never failed to critique my creations—all of these moments came rushing back with every ingredient I touched. One particular item held a special place in my heart—Hawaiian rolls. Jesse had a deep-seated love for these sweet, fluffy rolls, and I made sure always to have them on hand. I can still see his face lighting up with delight as he bit into a fluffy roll fresh from the package, his eyes twinkling with happiness.

Cooking became a form of communion, a way of staying connected to him through the rituals we once shared. In the rhythm of chopping, seasoning, and tasting, I found relief—a temporary rest period from the overwhelming grief that my wife and I were experiencing. Through the act of cooking, I discovered the therapeutic power of food—the ability to nourish not only the body but also the soul. Each meal prepared was a labor of love, a witness to the enduring bond I shared with my son, and a tangible expression of my grief.

Once a place of joy and togetherness, the kitchen had become a sacred space—a respected ground where I could commune with Jesse's memory and find moments of fleeting comfort amidst the storm of sorrow.

Embracing Fatherhood and Redefining Masculinity

This chapter in 'Out of Order' is not just my story—it's a shared experience of the strength of fatherhood, transcending labels, and genetic ties. It speaks to the universal experience of loss and the profound impact of true love.

To all stepfathers who have endured the heart-wrenching journey of saying goodbye to a child they did not birth, I want you to know that your pain and grief are valid, and your emotions are valid. As fathers, the love we carry for our children—stepchildren, adopted children, or biological children—is a timeless and unbreakable bond that transcends the constraints of conventional parenthood.

The journey of grief can be a solitary one, if not mindful, especially for men conditioned to conceal their emotions behind a mask of indifference. For all fathers, stepfathers, and father figures who have experienced the anguish of losing a child, remember that you are not alone. Let us break free from the constraints of traditional masculinity that dictate we must suffer in silence. In our collective sorrow, we can find power. Together, we can shatter the silence surrounding male grief and redefine masculinity to include the courage to mourn openly and authentically. By acknowledging and processing our grief, we honor fatherhood and pave the way for healing and growth.

For some men, the weight of societal expectations may often feel heavy, and we may be conditioned to conceal our emotions behind a disguise of indifference. But through my experience, I learned that vulnerability is not a sign of weakness—it is an indication of the depth of our love and the authenticity of our humanity.

Jesse's absence is a constant ache, a reminder of his profound impact on my life. As I navigate this journey of grief, I carry his spirit within me, an indication of the enduring power of love and the eternal connection between a father and his child, regardless of labels or biological ties.

Instead, let us create a space where tears are not signs of limitations but expressions of longing for a love that was once in this physical dimension. Together, we can rewrite the narrative surrounding male grief, fostering a culture of empathy, compassion, and mutual support.

Losing Jesse left me feeling exposed as if a vital part of myself had been ripped away. Yet, amid this anguish, I discovered a newfound strength—the strength to embrace my vulnerability, acknowledge the depth of my sorrow, and honor my son. In the wake of his passing, I navigated a whirlwind of emotions—grief, anger, confusion, and deep sadness. It was through embracing these feelings openly that I began to heal. I found relief in sharing my pain with others (colleagues, family, friends, and even strangers) who had walked similar paths and had had recent losses, realizing that my openness brought great inner strength.

Embracing Vulnerability

Through my own experience, I discovered that vulnerability is not an indicator of weakness—it is proof of my mortality. Combining that with listening to God's word was invaluable. The prophet Isaiah wrote, so do not fear, for I am with you; do not be dismayed, for I am your God. I will strengthen you and help you; I will uphold you with my righteous right hand. I had to believe God at His word.

Jesse's passing taught me invaluable lessons about embracing life with unconcealed passion and courage. He seized each moment in his brief time on this earth, leaving a lasting mark on everyone blessed to know him.

As his Pops, I am honored to carry Jesse's legacy through cherished memories by sharing meals and telling his story of strength, love, and the unwavering pursuit of dreams. Through the pain of loss, I have gained a deeper understanding of the true meaning of family—a bond constructed not by blood alone but by shared experiences, mutual support, and unconditional love. Jesse's passing has left an indelible mark on my life—a bittersweet reminder of the tenderness of existence and the enduring influence of love. As I continue to navigate this journey of grief, I carry Jesse's spirit within me, a guiding light that reminds me to live each day with purpose, but most of all with gratitude. His laughter echoes in the corners of my memory, a cherished melody that soothes my soul in those moments of sadness. Though he may no longer walk beside me, he remains forever in my heart—evidence of our eternal bond connected not through DNA but in TMV (through my vows).

I aim to start conversations about grief and resilience, empowering fathers to mourn openly with courage. When men witness other men mourning openly, it can provide a profound sense of validation and permission to express their own emotions freely. This redefinition of masculinity allows us to accept and process the stages of grief.

When asked to contribute to this book, my gut reaction was no. I'm not the type to be in the spotlight; I prefer staying behind the scenes. But then I thought about the importance of a father's voice, especially that of a non-biological father, and I knew I had to share my perspective. A view that many need to see is real and true.

> ***Proverbs 3:27-28 (NIV)****: "Do not withhold good from those to whom it is due, when it is in your power to act. Do not say to your neighbor, 'Come back tomorrow, and I'll give it to you'—when you already have it with you."*

My wife, in her grief in the days leading up to the funeral, said, "You don't understand; I gave birth to him." I know she was hurting, and while I can't feel precisely what she feels, my pain is real, and my loss is heavy. Jesse's life was deeply intertwined with mine. His joys, dreams, and struggles were all a part of my world. Jesse was my son in every way that mattered. I loved him deeply and losing him cut me to my core. It's a pain that doesn't have words, a loss that feels like a piece of my heart has been ripped away.

So, I decided to speak up for the dads who share my experience. There are so many fathers out there, stepdads, adoptive dads, and fathers of all kinds, who feel this profound loss but often stay silent because they think their grief is valid and they should take a backseat. But I'm here to tell you our love is strong. Our love, pain, and loss are all natural and meaningful.

Participating in this book was a way for me to comfort those walking the same path of grief and celebrate the beauty of fatherhood in all its forms. Fatherhood is more than biology. It's about the love and care you give, the memories you create, and the bonds you form. Jesse taught me much about life, love, determination, and resilience. His spirit lives on in every memory, every lesson, and every moment of joy we shared.

Through this book, I hope to provide a voice for dads who may feel in the shadows. I want to let them know that their grief is valid, their love is powerful, their role as fathers is invaluable, and it's okay to speak up.

I honor Jesse's memory and inspire others to embrace vulnerability, resilience, and the profound beauty of fatherhood. I also empower myself as a father. May our stories of love and loss serve as beacons of hope, guiding others through the darkest times and reaffirming the transformative power of love.

Together, we can heal and find strength in our shared experiences. Let's break the silence, support each other, and show the world that real manly strength comes from openness about love and compassion for others while they heal.

Willie Don Jackson III is the visionary behind Kingdom Influence, a nonprofit organization based in Michigan. As the founder, he spearheads the mission, vision, and goals of helping families, focusing on personal development and multi-generational literacy initiatives. Hailing from Muskegon, Michigan, Willie now calls Detroit home, where he continues to drive positive change and impact through his work for God.

He and his wife, Brigitte are the proud parents of eight children and thirteen grandchildren.

"There's no tragedy in life like the death of a child. Things never get back to the way they were."
-Dwight D. Eisenhower

AFTERWORD

My Dear Friends,

No one wants our story. God knows I didn't. I would've done anything to wake up one day and not have it be real, but that day never came. What did come was the opportunity to turn the page. By turning the page, I was able to see what God had for me moving forward, and my hopes and prayers are that as you heal, you gain the strength and clarity needed to be able to turn the page in your lives as well.

When navigating child loss, each step feels heavier than the last. But if you're reading this, it means you've made it one more day and for that, I am proud of you. I am proud of you for persevering through the waves of emotions that often seem insurmountable. This pain that we feel, though unwelcome, is a testament to the depth of love that we have for those we lost. Let's not shy away from it. It's natural—and indeed necessary—to lean into this discomfort, embracing every emotion that comes, whether it be sadness, anger, guilt, confusion, or even relief. Recognizing and naming these feelings diminishes their control over us and transforms overwhelming waves into manageable experiences. This is a crucial step as the ebb and flow of emotions happen in us.

The grief cycle, as outlined by Elisabeth Kübler-Ross, includes stages of denial, anger, bargaining, depression, and acceptance. This cycle is not linear; you may move between stages, experience them simultaneously, or revisit them over time. It's important to allow yourself to be in each stage as long as necessary, without rush or pressure. This requires a high level of awareness and, more importantly, the ability to manage it. Understanding this can offer a map through what might otherwise feel like uncharted emotional territory.

Managing your emotions through this process allows you to release. But here's the thing: that release has to be effective. Our emotions can often get the best of us, and we react in a way we don't want to. Our pain became the thing that had us emotionally hijacked. The effective release is like knowing the kettle is getting hot and ready to blow but having a release system for the pressure. If emotions stemming from grief are not expressed, they can build up and cause significant mental and physical health issues. Finding safe and healthy outlets for these emotions, whether through therapy, support groups, physical training, or spiritual practices, is essential. This release is about managing pain in a way that prevents it from overwhelming you, allowing you to reclaim control over your emotional well-being. Another critical thing to ensure you make a regular practice of is managing your self-talk.

Changing self-talk during this time is crucial. The narratives we tell ourselves can either anchor us further into the darkness of our despair or act as lifelines, pulling us toward the light. We must remind ourselves that it is possible to both mourn what was and still appreciate what is. We do this by honoring our children not just through our grief but through living a life that celebrates the time we had together.

The process of embracing grief is a challenge of both emotional and spiritual dimensions. To lean into grief is to accept it as a natural response to love lost, a significant part of your life that shapes but does not define you. It is now where you need to ask God to give again. For some of you, giving again could mean another child. For others, giving again can mean something that fills your heart. To get it, we must petition God for exactly what it is we want. Trusting God to give your "Samuel"—a purpose or passion that may emerge from endurance—is integral to this journey.

As we close, it is vital to acknowledge the absence left by your child. This empty space can never truly be filled, and it shouldn't be. Instead, let it be filled with God's presence, with love that transcends understanding, and with the peace that comes from knowing that love never truly leaves us; it merely changes form. Choosing to live fully in the face of child loss is about creating a legacy that honors the love and moments shared with your child, allowing yourself to experience joy, love, and peace without guilt.

As you turn each page of this journey of child loss, remember that healing is not about reaching a destination where the pain no longer exists but about learning how to carry it with grace, strength, and hope. Let each step be a testament to the love you hold and the growth you are capable of, even in the face of unimaginable loss.

Dimyas C. Perdue

Dimyas Perdue is a highly sought-after keynote speaker who is well-versed in guiding individuals and teams to achieve their full potential through emotional intelligence. His personalized leadership programs have earned him a reputation as a top-notch facilitator and his ability to inspire and motivate audiences is truly impactful. Dimyas Perdue is a true champion of personal and professional growth, and his expertise in helping with emerging leader programs has made him a valuable asset in the workplace and beyond. Dimyas has worked with foreign nationals such as the Jordanian Armed Forces, the Japanese Air Force, and the Philippine Marines. His multicultural competence, coupled with his facilitation techniques, are critical in helping teams develop strong partnerships and accomplish their missions.

Dimyas is the author of *Elevation Requires Change: The Journey Towards Purpose and Fulfillment* - the premiere book that empowers every heartbeat to unlock their potential and achieve true success.

Education:
Ph.D Candidate - Organization and Management,
Master of Arts, Human Services Counseling: Crises Response and Trauma.
Bachelors of Arts- Psychology: Military Resilience

Enhance Your Leadership Skills with Perdue Leadership Institute
Visit my website at: www.perdueleadership.com

"One of the major keys to success is to keep moving forward on the journey, making the best of the detours and interruptions, turning adversity into advantage."

-John C. Maxwell

THE FLIGHT ASSESSMENT

Why You Need the Flight Assessment

During tough times like losing someone special, Emotional Intelligence (EQ), which is the ability to understand and manage our own feelings while also understanding the feelings of others, is like a superpower we need to possess, develop, and sharpen.

In the Introduction, we stated that book contributors Ernie Cason, Dimyas Perdue, and Brigitte Jackson are certified trainers affiliated with Extreme Execution, a service provided by Thomas & Thomas Consulting, LLC. In this section we break that down more and have listed some possible ways each behavior preference may appear during grief.

If you'd like to know more about the Flight Assessment and how it can help you navigate your life these coaches can assist you and connect you with personal development support.

Understanding how you and others respond emotionally can make a difference when grief strikes. That's where knowing your personal tendencies comes into play. The Flight Assessment can help you see how you naturally react to tough situations like loss. But it's not just about you. Understanding your behavior preferences can help you support others who are grieving.

For instance, if you lose someone you care about and you are someone who likes to take charge and solve problems, like a decisive behavior style in the Flight Assessment model , self-awareness helps you realize that while you want to fix things, your friends might need something different. Your interactive behavior style field might need someone to talk to and do some fun things to feel better. Your stabilizing behavior style friend might need things to stay the same for a bit, or your cautious behavior style friend may want to analyze their feelings quietly. By using your self-awareness and knowing what you know about the Flight Assessment behavior preferences, you can get the support you need.

Knowing your tendencies can help you offer the right kind of support to others, making the grief process a little easier for everyone involved. Empathy in action. Knowing your behavior preference is like having a cheat sheet to help guide you through the difficulties of grief, both for you and those you care about. Using emotional intelligence, we can help each other through tough times like grief and mourning, ensuring everyone feels heard and understood.

**We have all four styles, but one may stand out more than the others. The charts on the following pages are only concepts to consider. There are variables that may influence this information. Reach out to an expert for a detailed analysis or to identify your style or preference.*

***The Flight Assessment is the proprietary property of Thomas and Thomas Consulting, LLC.*

Interactive Behavior Style

1. **Seeking Friends**: They go to friends for comfort when they're sad.
2. **Talking a Lot**: They talk a lot about their feelings.
3. **Using Art**: They might draw or write to deal with sadness.
4. **Being Social**: Being with friends and doing fun things helps them feel better.
5. **Needing Support**: They want others to say it's okay to be sad.
6. **Helping Others**: They help others even when they're sad themselves.
7. **Celebrating Memories**: They might organize events to remember the good times.
8. **Using Humor**: They make jokes to feel better.
9. **Being Thankful**: They focus on the good times they had with the person.
10. **Honoring the Person**: They might start a charity or fund to remember the person.

Stabilizing Behavior Style

1. **Keeping Routine**: They stick to their normal schedule to feel better.
2. **Listening to Others**: They're good at listening and being there for others.
3. **Creating Traditions**: They start habits to remember the person.
4. **Not Liking Changes**: They struggle when things change because of the loss.
5. **Avoiding Arguments**: They don't like fighting, especially when they're sad.
6. **Helping Others**: They help others to feel better.
7. **Seeking Comfort**: They want others to say everything will be okay.
8. **Hiding Emotions**: They keep their feelings inside a lot.
9. **Taking Care of Others**: They care for others even when they're sad.
10. **Using Religion**: They might pray or go to church to feel better.

Cautious Behavior Style

1. **Understanding Feelings**: They try to figure out why they feel sad.
2. **Learning About Grief**: They read books or talk to someone to learn more about being sad.
3. **Making Plans**: They make careful plans to feel better.
4. **Growing Personally**: They think about how they can become better people after being sad.
5. **Writing About Feelings**: They write in a diary to sort out their thoughts.
6. **Being Practical**: They focus on practical stuff, like sorting out money.
7. **Seeing a Therapist**: They might go to a therapist to get help.
8. **Keeping Feelings Inside**: They don't show their feelings much.
9. **Creating Memories**: They make things to remember the person who passed away.
10. **Spending Time Alone**: They like to be alone to think and feel better.

Decisive Behavior Style

1. **Action-Oriented**: They might quickly do practical stuff when someone passes away, like planning the funeral.
2. **Taking Charge**: They often lead and try to control their emotions.
3. **Not Showing Emotions**: They may not show their feelings openly.
4. **Keeping Busy**: Keeping busy with tasks might help them deal with sadness.
5. **Physical Activity**: Doing sports or exercises can help them let out feelings.
6. **Setting Goals**: They might make plans to feel better.
7. **Finding Closure**: They want to finish grieving and move forward.
8. **Doing Something**: They might organize events to remember the person.
9. **Finding Solutions**: They look for ways to feel better.
10. **Thinking About the Future**: They focus on what's coming next.

NOTES

NOTES

NOTES

UBUNTU PRESS, LLC

C/O Exponential EduVentures, LLC
PO BOX 7238 Dearborn, MI 48121
Fax: (866) 279-4589
www.ubuntupress.com

www.ingramcontent.com/pod-product-compliance
Lightning Source LLC
LaVergne TN
LVHW010927110826
845149LV00013B/2510